FIRE OF LOVE

Cassandra Poppe

ISBN: 978-0-9984368-0-7

PRAISE FOR *FIRE OF LOVE*

"Fire of Love is one of the best books I have ever read. It will dramatically stir the embers in your heart to a roaring flame of love. No burden, heartache, or catastrophe is too heavy or too much for God. Travel along with Cassandra Poppe and her son Fulton on an unforgettable journey of tragedy, pain, enduring love, redemptive suffering, and peace. Their pain was so intense, you might be tempted to close the book at times. However, I encourage you to hang tight to their hands and keep going. Cassandra beautifully unveils what lies beneath the shards and ashes to reveal an exquisite discovery of the 'Fire of Love.' She gently prods us, 'Just keep your heart open to Him . . . and peace will eventually come.' You will be changed for the better by reading this book. I guarantee it."

~**Donna-Marie Cooper O'Boyle**, EWTN Host of several TV series, Speaker, Award winning author of more than twenty books including: The Kiss of Jesus and Feeding Your Family's Soul. www.donnacooperoboyle.com

"I originally 'met' Cassandra through her writing in 2010 and have long admired her commitment to both her faith and her family. Since that January 2013 day that forever changed the Poppe family's life, my profound respect for Cassandra and Jay Poppe has only grown and deepened. In Fire of Love, Cassandra recounts with gripping detail and heartrending emotion a devastating accident involving her precious young son Fulton and how her personal trust in God's will enabled her to withstand circumstances that would bring most of us to the brink of devastation. This book moves beyond the story of Fulton's tragic burning and into the realm of a spiritual treatise, examining both the 'before' and 'since' moments that have contributed to Cassandra's passion for God and our Church. Along with way, you'll meet one of my favorite superheroes, Fulton Poppe, and discover how God is calling each of us, even in moments of vulnerability, to find our own way to serve the world around us. Read this book not only to learn how one family has coped with the unthinkable and thrived, but how you too might ignite a fire of love in your own heart."

~**Lisa M. Hendey**, Founder of CatholicMom.com and author of The Grace of Yes

"Most of the time we ask the question, 'Why do bad things happen?' Cassandra Poppe responds in her memoir, Fire of Love, with 'How do we respond to the bad things—with love or despair?' Her authentic, riveting, and often raw recollection of her son, Fulton's fire accident is truly a universal story—of struggle, suffering, wrestling, love, and redemption. What the world needs sorely is hope in God's mercy and unfailing love. Poppe delivers in a beautiful but honest way. Prepare your heart and soul to accept the message God has in store for you through her journey."

~**Jeannie Ewing**, author of From Grief to Grace: The Journey from Tragedy to Triumph.

TABLE OF CONTENTS

ACKNOWLEDGMENTS

Thank you to Jay, my love and my rock, who supported me as I gave birth to this book.

To my beloved children who shouldered so much without complaint and came together with ready and willing hearts to do whatever was necessary to keep hearth and home running while I was away.

To Lisa Hendey and Heidi Hess Saxton who first encouraged me to share my story with the world.

To Michelle Buckman, whose time and talents helped me uncover the diamonds in the rough.

To the generous hearts at the Bedouin Shrine in Muskogee and the entire staff at Shriner's Hospital for Children in Galveston who, without all of you, our sweet Fulton would never have survived. You will forever be enveloped in our prayers!

To all the souls throughout the world who selflessly offered us your precious time, treasures, and talents, and lifted us up in prayer and made our burdens light.

And most of all, to St. Louis de Montfort, St. Theresa of Avila, and Our Lady—for the conversion you worked so hard to begin in my heart, that I learn to love Our Lord with the wild abandon and trustful surrender He so rightly deserves.

God is good. Always!

PREFACE

When I first began writing this book, it was merely a way for me to sort out all that had been revealed to me during the intense suffering that began that cold January day in 2013. But as I wrote, the beauty hidden beneath the pain was slowly revealed to me in a way that not only served as a balm to my soul, but to others as well.

No one can escape suffering. We must all carry our crosses throughout life. And when that journey ends, we have not relief but more suffering still. A crucifixion. A constant call to die to self for love of God. It is not an easy journey, this road to Calvary. But so very essential to our salvation.

Some have told me that, at times, my story was difficult to read. Especially for burn victims and their loved ones. And so out of a deep respect for all those who have suffered in similar ways, please read my story with care, as some of my memories may remind you of your own sufferings. It is not my intention to excite one's imagination with horrific details. Rather, I want to let my readers realize that no matter how intense the suffering may be, there is always hope and even joy to be found along the way to make such crosses infinitely easier to bear. And that God's great love rises victoriously above all trials that come our way.

I am by no means a theologian, nor am I a scholar. And the lessons I have learned are tainted by my human nature and perhaps sometimes my flawed interpretations. Therefore, I have relied on Scripture and the wisdom of the Saints to help me sort out some of the harder lessons and say things that I may not be able to express as well as they. Most quotes I have used are commonly attributed to the holy souls I cite throughout the book, although at times it has been difficult to find their original source. And while it certainly helps to know that a Saint has offered us these nuggets of wisdom, the words still ring true no matter from whose lips or pen they first came forth.

Fire of Love is not an academic study on suffering. Nor is it a prayer book for those seeking solace. It is simply a story of a little boy, his mother, and the infinite love of God Who loved them enough to show them a better way to suffer by not only accepting suffering but actually embracing it for all the good it holds, by accepting His permissive will as we endure indescribable agony with the childlike trust that in the end we might begin to understand how much He loves us.

Fire of Love is a profoundly personal story, yet touches on the universal truths in such a way that any suffering soul might find some comfort, if only they learn to trust. God wishes nothing more than the salvation of our souls. And so it is through this lens of love—of God's divine providence in our lives—that I offer this work to you in hopes that you will open your hearts to the possibility that whatever you are suffering or will suffer in the future, you will be assured that beneath the pain, He has hidden for you a glimpse of His marvelous love and the glories to come.

Thy will be done, Lord. Thy will be done.

SECTION 1

A Life Lived

CHAPTER 1

*"For he is my God and my saviour: he is my helper,
I shall not be moved."*
—Psalms 61:8

The sky hung gray over our farm, considering whether it would dampen our plans or let us be. As the clouds vacillated, an occasional breeze stirred, cold enough to remind us it was January but not so cold that it would freeze fingers and make for clumsy work. Regardless of the weather, though, our plans for the day were going forward.

"Hold still, wiggle worm," I teased as I zipped up Fulton's fleece jacket. "It is chilly outside." He scrunched up his face with impatience as I finished my inspection. "Are you ready to help your daddy? It's a big day!"

"Yep!" he grinned, proud at the prospect of spending the morning doing 'men's work.' His blue eyes sparkled and his entire body was almost bursting with the kind of energy only a four-year-old boy can possess. I kissed his soft cheek, still smelling faintly of peanut butter and syrup—his favorite waffle topping.

"Get on out there!" I rustled his shaggy, ash blonde hair as he zipped away from me, his Lightening McQueen shoes making a soft *swoosh* sound as he headed to the front door. He was off to do men's work that morning, gathering sticks for the burn barrel and watching my husband Jay and his older brothers catch and skin our chickens.

As the door shut behind Fulton, the life our family had led was also closed to us forever. Had I known that would be the last time I would see my son's precious little face as it was, I would have taken the time for one last caress or a lingering gaze as he vanished from my sight. Or would I have even let him go outside at all? Perhaps, like Sleeping Beauty's father, I would have whisked him away that day, removing all possible dangers from him, trying to desperately defeat that which was to come. But alas, ignorance was bliss and there was the sink and counters to sterilize, tubs of salted ice water to fill, towels and freezer bags ready and waiting. It was chicken processing day, and I was too busy with the practicalities of our project to worry about the dangers.

The moment Our Lord redirected our lives that fateful January morning, I felt it more than I heard it. That deep percussion-like boom one hears when a firework is sent skyward, before it explodes. This was immediately followed by Jay's unintelligible cry.

Inwardly, I groaned as I saw patches of grass burning outside the window. *A grassfire. Lovely.* I paused a moment, deciding whether to continue on with my own preparations or poke my head outside.

Suddenly, Virginia, our 16-year-old daughter, burst into the kitchen. "Mom!" she screamed, "Fulton's on fire!"

"What?!" Flying back to the window, I looked to the side and saw what will haunt me forever. My four-year-old little boy was slowly moving away from the burn barrel, completely engulfed in flames from his waist to his head. His hands were clenched at his sides, moving them up towards his face in slow motion, pieces of his fleece jacket peeling away and falling behind him.

I ran to the pantry door. *Stop, drop and roll. Stop, drop and roll. He doesn't know stop, drop and roll!* I was wearing a long, loose sweater. *Could I smother the flames with this flimsy cloth? Or would that catch on fire and add to his injuries? What do I do?*

I flung the door open. By then, Jay was already on top of our son, Fulton's terrified screams muffled beneath Jay's body. While living in the country has a multitude of benefits, one major drawback was the lack of immediate emergency services. We lived half an hour away from the nearest hospital, and depending on where the ambulance was, it could take almost that long just to get an ambulance to our home. How much time would Fulton have? "911 or drive him in?" I yelled, trusting Jay would know what was best.

"Call 911," he boomed back. "Now!"

"Mary, Mother of God, please help us!" I prayed aloud as I dialed the phone.

I will humbly admit, when I spoke on the phone, I was not as calm as I would have liked to have been. Rather, I was terrified. "My son is on fire!" I screamed. The operator calmly asked a few questions which helped me regain my composure, and somehow I was able to relay enough information to her to allow her to do her job.

I have a vague recollection of staying on the phone with her but I think that is more of an assumption than a memory. When Jay carried Fulton into the house, all my attention was immediately directed towards him. "Mom," Virginia came to me, "There is a man at the fire station. Should I go get him?"

That was a miracle in itself. We lived right across the street from the volunteer fire station, but no one was ever there unless they had a meeting or were gathering to go out on a call. "Yes! Go!" I directed.

Jay gently laid Fulton on the kitchen floor at my feet, then quietly receded from view.

Meanwhile Fulton was shrieking in terror, looking wildly around him, unable to focus on anything. The rest of his clothes had burned away. He was dressed only in his underwear, with what was left of his dark blue pants still around his ankles. He trembled with both fear and cold. The stench of gasoline, charred flesh and burnt hair assaulted my senses. I almost wretched.

The man from across the street appeared and someone directed my daughter to get a clean sheet. We laid the sheet on the floor and moved Fulton onto it. He was still panicking and repeated over and over again, "Mama, I don't want to be on fire anymore! I don't want to burn!" His cries drew my heart to his in an inexplicable way—as though we were two parts of a whole. I wept internally with him, but would not let him see.

I knelt on the floor in front of him as he sat, his knees pulled up to his chest, looking wildly into my eyes. Calm instantly washed over me. "Fulton, look at Mama." I repeated this a few times until our eyes met. "Fulton, you are not on fire anymore. Daddy saved you, honey. You are going to be OK." Every time his eyes left mine, he started to panic again, so I kept him focused.

"Can you feel my hand?" I placed it on his left knee, the only major part of him that didn't appear to be burned. "Just focus on the feeling of my hand, Fulton. This knee does not hurt, OK? Think about your knee." I don't know if any of that really helped him, but it made me aware how much of him was actually injured.

There was a large patch on his right calf that was severely burned with smaller burns here and there on his leg. When his clothes caught fire, the elastic waistband of his pants melted into his skin and his waistline looked like bubbling, ground up flesh. There were patches of burns on his chest, his sides and his entire left shoulder blade matched his waistline.

Crying, he raised his arms to me, asking me to hold him, but as he did so, long strands of burned flesh hung down from his forearms, wrists and fingers like a partially unwrapped mummy emerging from its grave. New terror struck him, and he started frantically pulling at his flesh. "What is that?!" he screamed.

"Honey," my mother said from behind me, "I think those are just pieces of your burned shirt. Don't pull on them, OK?"

Thank you, Mom. "That's right, Fulton. Don't pull on that right now. We can get that taken care of later." But this new awareness of his burns caused him more anxiety. He needed to calm down. "Brave breaths, Fulton. Let's do brave breaths!" He nodded and within just a few slow, deep breaths, our breathing was synchronized and he was calmer.

We invented brave breaths when he was a toddler because of his tendency to overreact to the normal cuts and scrapes of boyhood. Any time I had to clean a wound or remove a bandage, we would take brave breaths together to help him cope with the pain. This familiar coping mechanism would come to be a major help in his healing over the next few years, and I was so thankful we already had it in place.

As we were doing our brave breaths, I tried to keep him focused on my eyes. It was the first time I allowed myself to actually take in the damage to his angelic face. His eyes, miraculously, were unharmed, save for his singed eyelashes. He had used his fists to cover his eyes, and this instinct helped salvage most of his eyelids and the raccoon-like patches around each eye. But the rest of his face did not fare so well.

The front of his neck was mercifully spared, but the collar of his shirt burned through his skin from under each ear and all around to the back of his neck, even exposing what looked to be burned muscle under his right ear. His cheeks and nose were a patchwork of charred skin and large, bloody blisters, yet his forehead looked eerily perfect. For an instant, I was relieved. But as I looked closer, his perfect looking skin took on a nauseatingly cadaverous look and I worried more about that skin than the rest of his face. His ears had the same waxy, death-like gray color. I had never seen a second or third degree burn before, but knew what I was looking at was severe.

I cannot even comfort him. Any other day, any other wound, he would be cradled in my arms as I rocked him, stroking his hair and wiping his tears. But that day I dared not touch him anywhere but his knee, fearing if I caressed his face it would dissolve in my hands and he would be lost to me forever.

His head had patches of hair, curled and black at the ends, and smears of fluid filled blisters and oozing skin. *Oh Lord, look at his skin!* I tried for a moment to imagine what sort of care he would require. *What will this mean?* It was too much for me to process all at once, and so we continued with the brave breaths until help arrived.

I vaguely recalled the first responders entering our kitchen. A bag or two of medical equipment. Lots of movement. Walkie-talkies. But for me, I was completely engrossed in watching my son's eyes. For the first several minutes they were wild with panic—darting to and fro, full of life and fight. But slowly the clearness of his eyes seemed to give way to a thick, dull coating and his eyes went from blue to gray. *Don't leave me, Buddy!*

One of the first responders immediately got down on the floor with us and began talking to him. "May I say a prayer for your son?" she asked. I nodded, thankful for her presence of mind and her ability to put into words that which I could not. "Fulton," she smiled, "I am going to say a little prayer with you, OK?"

Up until that moment, all I could say inside was, "Dear Lord, please help him. Save my Fulton. Mother Mary, pray for us." I could go no further than those short yet powerful prayers. Later, I would learn, there would be plenty of time for longer prayers. But for that moment, my simple cries for help would be enough. And while the words and tone of this woman's prayer were unfamiliar to me, I knew our hearts were lifted up to Our Lord in complete union.

Finally the ambulance arrived. The rest of the first responders wheeled the stretcher in and they gently laid Fulton upon it. By this time, he had grown much quieter, and only mildly protested as they moved him and made him lie down. As soon as the 911 dispatcher understood what the emergency was, she had immediately called for helicopter transport. And by this point, the chopper was already waiting for us just a few miles down the road on a school playground. They had to move quickly, the medics explained, before he went into shock.

"Mom, you're coming with us," one of the paramedics said as the last of the safety belts were in place. My mother had already gathered a few things—granola bars, a packet of Kleenex, $20, and her cell phone. Virginia knew to grab my rosary and had everything ready for me in a bag. The wheels bumped and the stretcher rattled as they swept him out of the house and down the porch steps.

For the first time since I saw Jay laying my son at my feet, I searched out my sweet husband. He was pacing in our living room, arms held up and away from his body as if surrendering. His clothes were burned and I could see his hands and arms were scorched. Our eyes met as I came to him, and he just shook his head. Tears streamed down both our cheeks. I caressed his face in my hands and kissed his lips, as he whispered, "No. Just . . . no."

"I love you," I whispered.

He turned his face away, trembling.

"I love you," I said again.

Still unable to meet my gaze, he rasped, "Be with him. Go!"

I ran to the waiting ambulance, shaken by the state Jay was in but unable to do anything for him. The plan was for my mother to take him to the nearest hospital in Arkansas for treatment and they would make the three hour trip to Tulsa as soon as he was released. Meanwhile, our 18-year-old son Ryan would follow the ambulance to the where the helicopter waited and take me to Tulsa once they took off. Virginia, Shannon, CJ and Marialina would remain at home until they could be taken to Tulsa with Jay later that day.

With the basic plans laid, we headed to the school. I rode in front with the driver but longed to be with my son. No specific prayers came to me at that point, rather fragments of my faith that came to my mind, sent from my heart as pleas to Heaven. *Jesus, Mary, Joseph . . . Please help us. Fulton Sheen, please save my son . . . Remember, O most gracious Virgin Mary, that never was it known that anyone who fled to thy protection, implored thy help or sought thy intercession was left unaided . . . Thy will be done.*

Suddenly, one of the paramedics banged on the partition behind my head. The ambulance stopped. "Don't worry," the driver soothed, "they are just trying to stabilize him." Somehow these words did not offer me the comfort he was trying to convey. And so the prayers continued.

To thee do we cry, poor banished children of Eve. To thee do we send up our sighs, mourning and weeping in this valley of tears . . .

The medic banged on the partition again, signaling that it was safe to move, and we continued on our journey. As the prayers flowed from my lips, I was inexplicably reassured. *You've got this,* I told myself. *You have been preparing for this. The Lord will see us through.*

Hail Mary, full of grace, the Lord is with thee . . . I believe in God, the Father Almighty

Yes. I believe in God.

CHAPTER 2

"Far better it is for you to say: 'I am a sinner,' than to say: 'I have no need of religion.' The empty can be filled, but the self-intoxicated have no room for God."
—Venerable Fulton J. Sheen

I believe in God.

It is a belief hard won, through many tears and prayers, a great grace finally bestowed upon me when I needed it most.

Those early years leading up to Jay's and my marriage certainly gave me no reason to believe there was a God who could possibly care for me. I wasn't even a likeable person. I had lived a life of openly mocking the teachings of the Catholic Church and focused on a life dedicated to self-worship. Whatever felt good was good. I had no long term goals beyond obtaining all things that brought me pleasure.

For several years, I actually thought I was happy. I reveled in a life lived by my own rules and ambitions, seeking both money and attention in all the wrong ways. It was all my will. My way. Always. Or so I thought.

I wouldn't even bother mentioning my unfortunate past except that the pattern of God's will trumping my own had played a powerful part in bringing me to the Catholic faith and ultimately bringing me the grace of accepting God's will hidden within Fulton's tragic accident.

This sense of peace that carried me through the tragedy is what amazed other people, and I am continually asked how such peace could be possible. Because it was such an amazing journey, as all conversion stories are, I willingly share it to show others how good our God truly is, and how He uses all things to bring us to a deeper trust in Him.

Looking back, I can plainly see many divine interventions Our Lord set in motion for Jay and me to meet, and then ultimately to convert to the Catholic faith. Truly, He put in my path many angels in disguise. However, at the time, I simply was enjoying the bizarre turn of events that seemed to be coming out of nowhere.

My first four years of life were spent on the beaches of Chicago, but the polluted city air and free-love attitudes of those around us pushed my parents to relocate our family to the country. They found a humble house on almost an acre of land in a tiny town called Alden. The home itself had an interesting past which may or may not have had a significant part to play in my life. For while the house itself had the typical storybook country charm, there was a darker side to it. The master bedroom walls were covered in Satanic symbols, and the owner went insane as my parents were finalizing the purchase of the house. But the real estate deal finally went through, the symbols simply painted over, and country life began for us.

Our family life was modest and blissfully normal, and I was secure in the love of my family. Nevertheless, there was always a sense of heaviness around me as a child that I could never identify. This feeling kept me up at night, terrified in the darkness and quiet that pressed in on me. Maybe it was simple childhood fears, or perhaps a presence in the house that haunted me. I cannot say for sure. But whatever the reasons, this darkness seemed to stay with me, even years after we moved away.

My parents had me baptized as a Catholic when I was an infant, and our family lived a little of our faith throughout the year. We said grace before dinner, observed Lent, Christmas and

Easter, and even celebrated St. Patrick's Day with a flair. I was raised to embrace my Irish heritage, inherited by my mother's side of the family, and was taught more about my Catholic faith in the few stories I was told about the potato famine than I had ever learned anywhere else.

Unfortunately, I lived most of my life rebelling against the faith in which my parents tried to raise me.

Mass was merely a place we went most Sundays, but for reasons I never really understood. It seemed to me to be a useless exercise. A perfect product of poor catechesis, any religious training I received simply confirmed in me that I was loved no matter what I did and there was no need to change. Each religion ultimately worshipped the same God, or so I was taught, and there seemed to be no urgency to belong specifically to the Catholic faith, or even any faith at all.

Sadly, I remember nothing of my First Communion, but I do recall my first confession. Slowly, solemnly, the priest and I ascended the steps of the sanctuary. We faced each other, sitting in the priests' chairs behind the altar in our church. The yellow painted walls did nothing to calm my jitters, and after I mentioned a few random sins I had committed, I took a deep breath and confessed the biggie: "When I was about three," I told Father, haltingly, "I got angry with my sister and broke my wooden horn over her head." It was not even an offense I remembered committing, but my sister and parents seemed to enjoy the retelling of this story. And if I did it, I concluded, I must confess it.

The absolute shock on the priest's face terrified me. His look said it all. My CCD teacher had lied to me and I realized right then and there that there were indeed some sins too horrible to even confess. *But how could I figure out which ones they were?* Panic set in. I quickly rattled off the rest of the wretched sins I had committed in my first seven years of life and left the church utterly changed. I knew I made a mistake confessing my sin that fateful day—the sin I did not actually remember committing. The instrument of my destruction. Confusion reigned and there was no peace for me.

Soon, this feeling of separation grew into an unnatural distaste for the Mass in general, and I happily missed it whenever I could. As Our Lord was raised above the priest's head at Mass, and while everyone else would pray, "Lord I am not worthy to receive You . . ." I would clench my little fists and silently rage against any indication that I was a sinner at all, defiantly refusing to acknowledge my unworthiness to receive Our Lord's True Presence. "I am worthy!" I would insist. And I would receive.

I only went to confession about three more times between my First Reconciliation and my high school years.

Confirmation training was no better than my First Communion training had been. My ignorance was so palpable, I did not even understand why we had to choose a Confirmation Saint. Or even what a Saint was.

"Which Saint have you chosen for your Confirmation?" Father asked me, one week before I was to receive the Sacrament.

"Mother Theresa!" I proudly answered.

He blinked a few times, and I knew once again I had made some horrible mistake. *But how could that be? She was the only person I knew of who seemed to live a life of charity. Wasn't that what we were going for here?*

"Umm . . ." Father stammered, "You need to choose someone who is dead."

Oh.

Awkward.

He had pity on me and said, "Perhaps you will like Saint Theresa of Avila. Do you know anything about her?"

I shook my head. St. Patrick and St. Nicholas were the only other Saints I had heard of.

"St. Theresa of Avila lived a life trying to become perfect. She always strove for perfection in everything she did. Does that sound like someone you could be inspired by?"

Perfection? Absolutely! For I, too, was on the path to perfection. Or so I thought.

Eighteen months earlier, we had moved from our small-town country life to an affluent suburb of Chicago. I was in a constant state of despair in junior high, and unable to pinpoint the source of my anxiety, so my parents decided we had to make a drastic move to help me heal. I had wanted that move to be the moment I would change my life forever. No more awkward and ugly. No more unpopular. No more misery.

But that first year and a half proved to be a disappointment. I was still ugly and awkward. I was still unpopular. And I was still miserable. Only now, instead of being all those things in a tiny classroom of eighteen students, I was now a nerd in a freshman class of over fifteen hundred in a town that thrived on living a life of affluence and good looks. It was a total culture shock to my system. Add to that Father's comment on striving for perfection.

Something clicked.

I would call it a lightbulb moment back then, but truly it was the switch that turned out any lights that remained. As a result, darkness engulfed me for several years thereafter.

Surrounded by this darkness, I suddenly had a plan. I had to perfect myself. I had dreams. Big dreams. And no shell of a nerdy goof with glasses was going to stop my inner self from achieving them. The time had arrived to cast off that shell and be who I felt I truly was inside.

I envisioned and I planned the rest of that year, and over the summer I worked on my makeup and wardrobe. I practiced my laugh, my smile, and plotted how to attract the attention of whomever I thought would help me morph into the person I wanted to be.

While I had never been overweight, my junior and senior years were dedicated to losing as much weight as possible. I dyed my hair Barbie-doll blonde, became very outgoing and actually changed myself enough to be considered very attractive in the eyes of most people. I had a few good female friends in high school with whom I managed enough mischief to keep my parents on their toes without getting into the kind of trouble that attracts too much attention.

Unknown to them, I was steeped in mortal sin.

By college, I thought I had learned enough to figure out what I wanted in life. Being a product of the late 1980s, I thought I wanted it all. Materialism gripped my heart and became my idol. Having such an idol in my heart demanded that I focus my energies on who I needed to become to obtain that which I desired most. I began severing the last ties I had with people outside my family who truly cared for me. I knew I did not deserve them or their love, but at least I had a plan for worldly comforts, if I played my cards right. And this somehow was an acceptable compromise. The scheming and busyness of what my plans demanded helped hide the true loneliness and unworthiness eating away at my heart.

Meanwhile, my mother was growing concerned that I had no girlfriends, so she encouraged me to join a sorority, a move that did not help me with all I wrestled with inside. I seemed to have an inability to connect with other females in my life. Truly, if I could have joined a fraternity, I think it would have been a better fit, because it was only when I was surrounded by males that I felt any confidence at all.

My grades were abysmal, and I left after two years, still nurturing big dreams. I got a job as a cocktail waitress in a Jazz club frequented by the very rich and used that to boost my lifestyle. The tips were large and invitations to a better life were frequent. *Baby steps towards the perfect life*, I thought. But in reality they were huge leaps further into Hell.

I truly regretted the hearts I broke along the way, and even made a few honest attempts at real, meaningful relationships. I loved as best I could, but I was unable to love completely. Resigned to the fact that love must not be something for me to enjoy, I continued on the path towards destruction, a path that was about to lead me into a world from which I would probably never have recovered, had not my Guardian Angel finally stepped in.

***

Jesus, meek and humble of heart, make my heart like unto thine!

CHAPTER 3

*"Beside each believer stands an Angel as protector
and shepherd, leading him to life."*
—St. Basil the Great*

There are times when a soul is drawn to its knees, and begs the Lord to pull it out of its misery—a treasured grace. But it was not for me. For there are other souls who are so miserable, they are blind to the chains that bind them. These souls need to be rescued in a more immediate manner, not wasting time for a repentant heart to come around. Sadly, that was my story.

By this time, I was living in an apartment on the Gold Coast in Chicago, working in fashion retail. On a morning when I should have been sleeping late, I suddenly woke up in a panic. *I'm going to be late!* Leaping out of bed, I frantically showered and dressed, not even bothering with makeup. *I'm late!* Only later did I attribute this abrupt beginning to my day to my Guardian Angel, for indeed, if I had not responded as quickly as I did that morning, my life would be very different now. And not for the better, I am sure.

Out the door I went, headed who knows where. It was a cold fall day, but sunny, and realizing that I really had no idea where I was headed, I decided to visit a statue that I was in the process of purchasing from an art gallery. The price was a bit beyond my means, but I was so taken by it, I just had to have it.

It was a statue of St. Michael, the details so perfect, the movement within the sculpture so powerful, it was as though it was actually St. Michael himself. That statue was angel number two.

I entered the gallery and was warmly greeted by the store manager, who actually shared a name with an angel. "Good morning," I said to her, unbuttoning my coat. "Just stopping in to say hello to Michael."

"Oh! You are just in time!" she said excitedly. "You know, the son of the artist who created your statue is here. Do you want to meet him?"

This meeting turned into a discussion over coffee, a late night phone call, and ultimately a job offer.

Aha! That must be what I was late for that morning! I was supposed to meet this man so I could get another job! I had always listened to those inner urgings and I was glad I once again followed my instincts that morning.

I graciously accepted and began my new career as an art gallery saleswoman. Sooner than what would have been seen as normal, Angel announced that she was being transferred to Denver. "Would you like to join me?" she asked. "They have a sales position for you in the Colorado gallery if you want it."

I wanted it. And so I went. I left behind some very confused sisters, parents, and friends who were wondering what I was doing. But they had also grown accustomed to my rather erratic behavior, so they said nothing and decided to simply sit back and watch.

The Colorado gallery was far different from the gallery I left, and business was sparse. And before long, I was let go. So there I was, a Chicago girl completely out of her element, all alone, and desperate. I had always relied on working in bars in the past to make a lot of cash quickly, so I scanned the papers to see who was hiring. I decided on a sports bar that was just about to open, figuring opening business would be good and I could establish myself early on with the customers.

I was hired. But after a week of training, I found the bus schedule to be incompatible with my work schedule, so I asked the owner if my schedule could be altered. "Where do you live?" he asked.

I told him the name of the apartment complex and he smiled. "Come here a minute."

He led me to the window where food was passed from the kitchen to the wait staff, and there towards the back of the kitchen was a young man expertly spinning pizza dough into the air. He was dressed in jeans and a T-shirt, his long auburn hair in a ponytail. I had never seen him before. "Jay!" the owner called, "I have someone I want you to meet."

Jay continued to work the dough back and forth between his hands as he approached, smiling. His red beard and mustache made me smile back. *Wow! A real rugged mountain man!* He certainly looked different from the usual men I knew.

"This is Cassandra. She lives in your apartment complex. You will be driving her to and from work every day. I'll make sure your schedules match."

Jay smiled a huge smile. "Sure!" he said. "Nice to meet you!"

It was not love at first sight. In fact, I didn't think much of Jay at all. I was still recovering from a broken engagement and wanted time to make more solid plans for myself. Meanwhile, Jay was a free ride to and from work, and very convenient to have around.

Before long, we were staying at the bar after our shifts were through. He made me all sorts of original, one-of-a-kind pizzas, a gift I truly appreciated as tips were miserable and I was hungry. We played pool and just had fun together. I never considered taking him very seriously, though, as there was nothing he could offer me that I thought I wanted. However, I had learned the hard way that people in Colorado did not tip nearly as well as they did in Chicago, and I was suddenly hurting financially. So when Jay asked me to move in with him, I said yes.

I didn't know that I was already pregnant.

I announced the pregnancy to Jay a few weeks later.

We fought. I cried. And we broke up.

I needed time to sell my things and get a train ticket back to Chicago as soon as possible. We were still living together for a few days after this decision was made, though, and the whole situation was very uncomfortable.

Jay was studying for his medical lab tech exams at the time, so when we were not working together, he stayed at a friend's house to study, keeping out of my way as best he could. Then one night, as I was finishing up my shift at the sports bar, he walked through the door. He looked like a complete wreck and his eyes were swollen. He strode directly to me, and I feared he was angry. *Oh please, just don't make a scene . . .*

"I can't concentrate on anything," he said. "Can we make this thing work? Somehow?"

I nodded my head in disbelief. That night we talked about our plans. They were not the kind of plans I had envisioned for my life. Not by a long shot. They were not even plans for a long-term future. But what could I expect?

"I have grown to care about you," he said, "and whatever you decide to do about this baby is up to you. But I want to let you know that I will do my best to support you in whatever your choice is."

He was honest, and I appreciated it. We both knew we did not love each other. By that point in my life, I do not think I was even capable of saying the word and meaning it, but I could handle honesty. It was a start.

"I want to go see a doctor. A real doctor. I'm not going to Planned Parenthood."

I had never felt easy in their offices in the past and somehow knew that would be a dangerous place for me. My Guardian Angel must have been hard at work to keep me from making a huge mistake during those precarious days, for which I am eternally grateful. Jay called his mother and got a name of a doctor in town, and I made an appointment to meet angel number four.

"Well, it looks as though you are indeed pregnant," the doctor announced with a smile. He shuffled some papers and filed them on his bookshelf behind his huge wooden desk, and casually asked, "So what are your plans?"

I hesitated. I seemed to swing back and forth in my mind whether to keep this child or seek an abortion. I didn't want an abortion, but I didn't see how any other scenario could play out to a happy ending. "I am thinking of maybe an abortion." Just saying the words out loud sounded dissonant to me, as though it went against every fiber of my being.

He turned towards his desk and sat down, a small, gentle smile still on his face. Not a sneer. No judgment. Just a genuine smile, which put me at ease.

"You do realize there are other options available, right?"

"Well, yes," I stammered. "But maybe not for me. I am just a waitress in a sports bar. I can't afford to raise a child on tips." Admitting this out loud seemed to solidify in my mind that I certainly could not keep my baby.

The doctor nodded. "And what does the father do?"

I cleared my throat, feeling awkward even discussing Jay. "He is a manager at the bar where I work. And he makes pizzas . . ."

"I see." He leaned forward. "And your plans for the future? Have you two reached the highest level in your careers yet?"

"Well, no," I almost chuckled, "I don't want to be a waitress forever. And he is going to graduate from a medical lab tech school in a few weeks. He even said he wants to become a doctor."

"Ah!" He sat back in his chair and the smile came back. "So your situation now will not be your situation six months or six years from now. Right?"

"Right." *Where is he going with this?*

"But this baby will be forever. Things, situations, can change very quickly in life. You have to focus on the forevers. It sounds like there is a promise of brighter days in your future. You just have to decide if that future includes your baby."

My heart pounded. *He is right! I was so wrapped up in the now, I had completely forgotten about the possibilities for the future. And my future could—no, must—include this child.*

"If you truly feel unable to care for your baby, I can refer you to some adoption groups that will help you with shelter, medical costs, and even placing your child for adoption."

I briefly allowed myself to consider this possibility. But my future was now opened up to me in a new way, and I understood what I was to do.

Suddenly feeling protective of my baby, I shook my head. "Thank you, Doctor," I grinned, "But I think I . . . we . . . can do this!"

We chatted for a few more minutes and he escorted me to the door. "Best of luck to you all," he said as he opened the door for me. I walked out to the waiting area. "Make sure you feed her well!" he called to Jay before returning to his office.

Jay stood up when he saw me, and waited expectantly. "Well?"

"We're having a baby!"

I later learned that during this time, many states away, my grandmother and Confirmation sponsor prayed nightly to St. Theresa of Avila and to Our Lord to return me to the faith. How grateful I am to her perseverance, for without her prayers, my life could have turned out very differently. May she rest in peace.

***

O Father, in the name of Your Son Jesus, and in the power and authority of the Holy Spirit, with the knowledge of Your will, I ask that You fill Cassandra with the knowledge of Your will through all spiritual wisdom and understanding.

Enlighten this precious child of Yours, dear Lord! Teach this dear one to live in a manner that is worthy of You, so as to be fully pleasing to You, full of good works bearing good fruits and ever growing in knowledge of You.

Strengthen this lost lamb, dear Lord, with every power of Your Holy Spirit, in accordance with Your might, for all endurance and patience, with joy, giving thanks to You, O Father!

Make Your child fit to share in the inheritance of the holy ones in the Light.

Deliver this beloved one from the power of darkness into the kingdom of Your Beloved Son, Jesus, and transfer Cassandra into the kingdom of Your Beloved Son, Jesus, in whom is redemption and the forgiveness of sins.

Amen!

—Traditional prayer for conversion

CHAPTER 4

"Because everyone that exalteth himself, shall be humbled: and he that humbleth himself, shall be exalted."
—Luke 18:14

Our decision to raise our child together was not a happy ending to our story, but simply a beginning of a new chapter.

Our lives were riddled with poverty and hardship, but once our baby boy arrived there was suddenly a space in my heart that had never before been opened, and I knew that no matter how difficult things became, this child, this treasure, would always be my joy. We both loved Ryan with all our hearts. We truly embraced parenthood and I had hoped eventually, this common bond of love would translate to a closer bond with Jay. Since I was no longer able to fall on any backup plans I might have had before the pregnancy, I knew I had to find a way to make things work between us.

We finally decided to get married when our son was a year and a half old, and I remember my incredible hesitancy to tie the knot. "Mom, I just don't love him. And I know he does not love me," I explained, miffed at myself for even considering marriage in the first place.

"Well, honey, that may come in time. He is such a loving father. He has a very strong work ethic and takes his responsibilities seriously. He is never angry and everyone loves him so much." I closed my eyes, trying to tune out the list of Jay's virtues that continued to assault me, but all I could picture was a circle of friends and family members throwing rose petals at his feet.

I think that was the problem—jealousy. Everyone loved Jay. He had the kind of personality to which people were drawn, and it was difficult for me to express any negative concerns about him with others. They just did not see what I saw. I myself could not put a name to the problem, but it felt deep and dark and it took every ounce of strength I had to resist the urge to flee. In the end, I resigned myself to a loveless but friendly marriage. We had no real love for each other, but we did love our baby. And that, we decided, was enough.

We married in a cabin in the woods in Wisconsin, my high school friend's father presiding. He was a Lutheran minister and was the closest thing to God I allowed myself to be near at that time. Our marriage was just a formality, solidifying our commitment to our son more than to each other. We said we loved each other that day, but we did not.

What should have been a happy day for me was truly miserable, and lying awake on our wedding night next to a man who scarcely attempted to even talk to me, I wondered at what point the surrounding darkness would actually consume me. Not only was I dead to the rest of the world, but I was dead to my husband as well. He continued to be the perfect father, the perfect son-in-law and brother-in-law. "You are so lucky to have him!" everyone would gush. "He's wonderful!"

I couldn't tell them of his painful rejection of me and his own inability to love. And so I just smiled in agreement and changed the topic of conversation. I didn't understand what was happening. All I could hope for was that one day he would finally change. Or vanish.

One night, a few months after the birth of our second child—a daughter, and after yet another bout of tears alone in my bedroom, I realized I couldn't make Jay love me. No matter what I did or what I looked like, I could never be who he wanted me to be. My entire house of cards, my entire teenage and adult life built on trying to be attractive to others, and to gain the upper hand, finally collapsed. The sheer weight of the truth set before me brought me to my knees, weeping. *Oh Lord, why?* But I was not yet ready for His answer.

I was in despair. No longer able to live the only life I once knew, and trapped in a loveless marriage, I was a complete wreck. I wanted a divorce. I wanted out so badly, my heart raged against Jay, never hating anyone as much as I hated him. I hit my knees in prayer—the first prayer I prayed in more than a decade—and sobbed. *Please, Lord. I have no right to ask anything of You, but get me out of this. I want out. This is not a real marriage, and I am miserable. Help me out of this Hell I am trapped in!*

I stood up, feeling suddenly stronger. I was determined to demand a divorce. Emboldened by this new sense of purpose, I felt that what I was about to do would be the first and best thing I had ever done for myself in my life. The thought of being released from him was almost exhilarating!

I stormed downstairs and found Jay on the couch, dozing in front of the TV with our baby girl asleep on his chest. "Jay!" I shouted, waking him from his slumber. I opened my mouth. But instead of demanding a divorce, the words, "We have to start going to church," fell from my lips.

I think I was more startled by my words than he. We talked. We cried. And he agreed.

To my amazement, Jay immediately embraced the Catholic faith, while I lingered in the shadows. I wasn't about to commit myself to yet another prison. I followed him reluctantly, thinking I already knew what was in store for us if we became one of 'those' families. You know. The families who went to Mass every Sunday, cooked lots of casseroles, and probably held Bible studies in their homes. For fun.

Quite frankly, I was still inwardly seething at Jay for the hurt he had caused me, and I still struggled mightily with pride, resenting Jay's enthusiasm for converting to Catholicism. I was angry over him willing accepting that he was forgiven for all his past sins, especially for purposely withholding love from me. I was angry his sins were not seen as unforgivable as the actions of a three-year-old and her broken wooden horn. I was angry that everyone in our church loved Jay so much. And I was angry at his joy. *Wasn't he, after all, the one who drove me to the brink of divorce? What right did he have to be so happy?* He still had a lot of explaining and apologizing to do before I could begin to embrace this new faith to which he was committing.

What I couldn't see was that I was so focused on how he had hurt me, I had never taken the time to consider my role in our failed marriage, and how I had offended Our Lord. I just was not yet ready for that kind of inner discovery. So, I continued on, a slave to my own pride and a willful spirit that continued to poison me.

Jay was working on becoming a better husband, but I felt like he should have been suffering. I guess I was hoping for some sort of punishment to come his way. A dose of justice to help even the playing field. So, I kept this poison circulating in my heart. *Where is Your justice?* I repeatedly demanded of God, until one Sunday morning I heard the following Gospel. Only I did not hear it as it was read. What I heard was this:

> *Luke 18:9-14: And to she who trusted in herself as just, and despised others, He spoke also this parable: A married couple went up into the temple to pray. The woman standing, prayed thus with herself: O God, I give thee thanks that I am not as my husband,*

unjust, cruel, and a liar. I gave up everything for him—my dignity and my life, and sacrificed myself for him. I deserve better than the life I have! Haven't I done enough? And the husband, standing afar off, would not so much as lift up his eyes towards heaven; but struck his breast, saying: O God, be merciful to me a sinner. I say to you, this man went down into his house justified rather than the wife: because every one that exalteth himself, shall be humbled: and he that humbleth himself, shall be exalted.

Ouch.

I realized, in those words, what a wretch I had been. I wanted to run out of the church, away from my family and away from God. Jay was truly amending his life in miraculous ways. Somehow God was calling him to repentance and conversion. And I was jealous. Jealous of Jay's joy, and jealous of the love to which Jay had opened his heart. And jealous that God's love was not for me.

But realizing this jealousy was within me did not enrage me as it would have before. Instead, it simply made my heart profoundly sorrowful. I realized for the first time how wretched I was. I was truly no better than he. Was my own calculating way of treating those who loved me any better? Using people in my past to keep me from feeling lonely, for money and a sense of twisted power and pride? By the end of Mass, I was truly a repentant sinner, head hung low, and ready to open my heart to the risk of being completely loved for the first time in my life. Loved by God.

This terrified me, because I knew that He knew every unlovable piece of me. In truth, there was not much left to love. I suddenly recalled my first Confession and recoiled at the thought. *If breaking a horn on my sister's head was a sin that bordered on unforgivable, what was I to do with the sins I had committed in the past decade? Would He reject me? Would I fail to live up to His standards?* I knew the risks, but no longer cared. My only other choice, of course, was death, and somehow I knew even that would offer me no relief.

I loved my children and did not want to lose them. And on a certain level, I was also growing attached to Jay as well. But at that moment, what I craved most was the love of God I had never before experienced. I wanted a tearful Hallelujah moment. I wanted dancing and tambourines. I wanted a miracle. And I wanted Christ.

Praise God for His patience with me, and for Jay's patience as well. For while Jay was trying to deal with my issues, he was also wrestling with his own demons, which weighed heavily on his soul. His journey to the faith is his own story to tell, but at one point, he shared with me a bit of his own private conversion, his conversion to love.

He had been driving to a home inspection, mulling over matters of the faith and his plans for the day, when a light hit him from within. He literally saw the Cross before him and he knew at last what it meant to love. To truly love. A sacrificial, suffering sort of love that changed his heart forever. Breathless, he pulled to the side of the road and absorbed its glory. And at that moment, he became a new man.

I am so grateful that God, in His great wisdom, knocked Jay off his donkey first, allowing him to be patient enough to gently lead me Home, giving me the time I needed to learn to trust and open my heart to God without fear. For even though I was baptized Catholic and received the Sacraments through the Church, I cannot say I am now a revert to the faith because to revert to the Catholic faith would imply I used to be a part of it. Indeed the Sacramental marks were upon my soul, but there was never at any time an outward sign of Catholicism in my life or within my heart. My faith journey had me covering ground I had never before walked upon, and I had no idea what to expect.

This was a trying period for Jay and me, and one for which I am most grateful. We learned a lot about each other, and about ourselves. We learned for the first time what it meant to truly love. We learned sacrifice. We learned that marriage could be difficult. We learned forgiveness. We learned to work together as one. And most importantly, we learned to put our trust in God.

On Easter 2000, after our third child was born, Jay was brought into the Catholic Church, and we surprised our RCIA group with an official blessing of our marriage. We finally had a Sacramental marriage and were ready to embrace our newfound love of the faith and begin to form true bonds of love for each other as well.

These lessons, hard learned, proved to be a fruitful training ground for other trials that were still to come. Each trial was a struggle, but we knew how to trust each other and trust the Lord to help us through. As we came through those difficulties, we were drawn a little closer as a family and perhaps a little holier as well.

Had we given up and gotten a divorce in 1998, we never would have come to the Catholic faith. We never would have given life to our other children. We never would have seen how much our loving and merciful God trusted us with His greater plans, or how trustworthy He could be.

***

As St. Margaret of Cortona once said, "In times of desolation, God conceals Himself from us so that we can discover for ourselves what we are without Him." And so I thank You, Oh Lord, for this path of humility You have set me upon. With You, I have hope at last. Without You, I am lost. Be with me always, and show me Your ways and Your will, and never let me stray from You again. Amen.

CHAPTER 5

"Look upon yourself as a tree planted beside the water, which bears its fruit in due season; the more it is shaken by the wind, the deeper it strikes its roots into the ground."
—*St. Margaret Mary Alacoque*

From the day I said we needed to start going to church to the day we had our marriage blessed, about 18 months had passed. A lot of issues were being ironed out at last, and Jay and I were truly beginning to fall in love for the very first time. My eyes and ears were opened, my heart softened, I was finally basking in post-conversion warmth. And through it all, I had learned a new word: faith.

But just like all conversion stories, our story did not end with our conversion. Our work had just begun! The book of the life we led before Catholicism was shelved for good, destined to gather dust. That life was over, and we were anxious to see what God had in store for us.

We didn't have long to wait.

By the beginning of 2001, Jay's home inspection business was flourishing and I was making a very comfortable salary working for a worldwide corporation editing technical manuals and preparing and tracking annual budgets for the computer department. We had a nice house in the suburbs and our oldest was enrolled in our parish's Catholic school. Jay and I were very much in love with each other, much to the envy of many we knew, and we were finally experiencing a taste of happiness we never thought possible. In our eyes, our life was perfect.

I remember standing one day in my bedroom, beautifully furnished and freshly cleaned by the housekeeper who worked for us a few days a week. Jay was playing with the children downstairs and I was changing for dinner. *Thank you, Lord, for my life. At last, I am truly happy and content. If everything stays as it is, I could be happy forever. Please, may nothing about this life ever change.*

Of course, soon after this heartfelt but admittedly selfish prayer, our lives began to change.

Since our conversion, we were abundantly blessed financially. And because of this, we grew lazy in our faith. We attended Mass on Sundays and I was beginning to make an effort to pay attention to a few feast days throughout the year. Jay and I began reading the writings of the Saints and Scripture, but our lives were still very much rooted in the world.

Then one Saturday morning as I was sorting laundry, I heard an inner voice tell me one word.

Prepare.

Prepare? For what? I shook it off and went on with my sorting. But then it hit me again.

Prepare.

Ok then. Prepare. Got it.

I brought the laundry upstairs, set the basket down and sat on my bed. I bowed my head and waited for a grand revelation to hit me. *Lord, if that was You, what would You have me do? What am I preparing for?*

Silence.

Unsure how long I was supposed to wait for an answer, I gave Him another twenty seconds and gave up. I had things to do and did not have time to mull over random verbs that popped into my head. So I tried to push the word aside and carried on with my day.

But several times that week the word kept coming back to me. Should I be preparing for some sort of natural or war-related disaster? Was something terrible going to happen to us? Or was I to prepare for something eternal? The business of life crowded out any further speculation, and I forgot the message.

Soon after, I was carrying within me our fourth child. As the pregnancy progressed, I found it harder and harder to imagine leaving yet another child behind every day to go to work. It would be difficult to quit my job, but through diligence and my little-known talent for creating financial spreadsheets, I had already eliminated almost $30,000 in credit card debt in less than two years. Aside from carrying a mortgage, we were finally debt free. Jay's business was booming. Could it be I was to prepare to stay at home with my children? I set the idea aside and thought I would 'pray about it' at a later date.

Then the tragedy on September 11, 2001 occurred. I was so rattled, I called in sick to work and spent the day glued to my mother's television. We had given up television in our home a few years earlier and did not miss it at all, but on this day I felt it was important for me to know what was going on.

I kept my hand protectively over the growing life within, terrified at what kind of future was ahead of us. The thought of having to leave my children to go to work now felt unbearable. *I could continue working until after the baby was born, and then I would come home for good.* I easily convinced myself it was the right thing to do. *Perhaps this was what I was to prepare for—a way to maintain our happiness as best we could, sheltered from the rest of the world. Why would Our Lord bring us to the faith, bless us so abundantly, and then let it slip away?*

Becoming a stay-at-home mother seemed like a reasonable answer to what my mysterious message was about, so Jay and I discussed it. It was not a hard sell for him; he knew how miserable I was in my job. We had just purchased a new van to fit our growing family and were comfortable with the payments we would have to make. Jay's company had just been bought out by a national home inspection company and we were guaranteed a healthy salary.

Not only that, but Jay had just started another side business which promised to be another successful venture. *God is so good*, I thought, *to continue to bless us. He has made it so I can stay at home with our children without making any sacrifices. Surely this was God's will!*

I struggled physically through the rest of my second trimester, and by the third trimester I was assigned to complete bedrest with medications to keep me from going into labor. I had similar difficulties with my previous pregnancy, so I was prepared to spend several weeks reading and sleeping. Our newfound Catholic friends kept a constant supply of home cooked meals rolling in and proved to me once again how blessed we were. No discomfort could touch us without a greater temporal blessing attached.

Unfortunately a form of spiritual pride took over, convincing me that Our Lord would provide for all our temporal needs, sheltering us from all discomfort. And why shouldn't He? We were Catholic! Obviously I was still very much in the baby stages of faith, as I did not realize what being Catholic was truly about. But Our Lord was about to prepare us for the harder lessons of faith of which we had yet to experience in our lives.

January 2002, our son Collin was born. Like all my labors, it was fast and beautiful and my happiness was complete, when, right after Collin was born Jay stood above us, placed his hands on our baby's head and tearfully prayed a prayer of thanks to God for blessing us with this child. His sincerity brought tears to my eyes, and I thanked God for this man, my rock, to whom I was married.

I gave notice at work a few weeks later and soon began my life as a stay-at-home mother. Not only did I stay at home, I started to homeschool as well. I dove right into this new, uncharted life of mine, convinced this was exactly what God wanted me to do. How could He not want it? I was so happy!

A few months later, though, I was about to embark on a very difficult journey, covering the surprisingly vast distance between happiness and joy.

"Cassandra, I have to prepare you for something," Jay announced one evening, "just in case something happens." *It couldn't be anything really bad*, I thought. *God is with us.* And so I awaited his news with calmness and serenity. "I think I am about to get fired."

Whoa. I did not see that coming! "What? Why?" As he explained the details, all my inner engines began to whir. *The mortgage. The new car payments. The money we owed on the equipment for his new venture. No job. No health insurance.*

"The owners of the company will be flying in on Wednesday. They will meet me for dinner and," he paused, "I think I am finished." The agony on his face snapped me out of my own thoughts and I gave him a hug. *Alright*, I concluded, *the Lord has a huge job opportunity just waiting for Jay and we will be better off than ever! This will be exciting!*

Of course I did not immediately offer him this bit of news. Jay wasn't ready. He did not believe God worked in the same way that I believed God worked. Jay believed that both good and bad things in life happened regardless of one's level of faith, and we were simply called to keep the Lord in our lives to help weather the storm and find ways to use those moments to grow in holiness. Silly man.

"We'll get through this together," I assured him. "Why are they firing you?"

In an effort to improve our lives even more, Jay had started another business on the side, eliminating homes of molds, mildew, and lingering odors. It was very "green," and very effective, and we were excited about the success this new venture promised to bring. He had the home inspection company's permission to run this side business along with the responsibilities he had with them, as long as he kept a distinct separation between the two and there was no conflict of interest.

I suppose we should have seen it coming. Jay inspected homes for a living, and he was bound to come across a home with mold. And so it happened.

The inspection for one particular house was going as inspections usually do, until they went into the attic. Mold. And lots of it. Jay pointed this out to his client and made a note of it in his report after explaining the possible dangers of living in a house with this particular type of mold in it. He was not allowed to pitch his extra services to any home inspection clients when he came across a problem—a rule he completely stood by. But the real estate agent who was attending the inspection with his client cheerily said, "Well, mold is not a problem, right Jay? You know how to get rid of that!"

Needless to say, the home owner was livid, assuming Jay called out the mold to double dip or ruin the sale of his home. The home owner called the home inspection company the next day, and when Jay's managers flew in to talk to Jay, the ax fell.

It was a sad parting of ways, as the owners and Jay had a wonderful relationship up to that point. Jay handled it with the social grace he always possessed and readily admitted he was playing with fire in trying to run both businesses. Humbled, and with no residual anger to hold him back, he was ready to tackle the challenge of finding a new way to provide for his family.

Meanwhile, I swung back and forth between anger at the homeowner who made the phone call and curious to see what would happen next. Jay was forbidden, by contract, to start up a new home inspection business in the Chicago area. He knew of no other trade that would give us the salary to which we had grown accustomed, so we had to consider the unthinkable—moving.

I took a deep breath. "OK. Where are we going?" I asked.

"Arkansas."

***

Lord, I thank You for the little lights You send my way to help keep me on the right path. Continue to prepare me in a multitude of ways for all that still lies ahead in my life. Keep me firm in my faith and close to You so that even if I do not have the wisdom to heed every calling, I will always, at least, strive to respond to Your will as best I can. Amen.

CHAPTER 6

*"There are in truth three states of the converted: the
beginning, the middle, and the perfection. In the beginning,
they experience the charms of sweetness; in the middle,
the contests of temptation; and in the end,
the fullness of perfection."*
—*Pope St. Gregory the Great*

"Arkansas?" Banjos were twanging in my head so loudly, I hardly heard his explanation.

"The cost of living is so much more affordable down there," he began, "and it's not like we don't know anyone."

That was true. We had visited Jay's sister and family a few times in Fort Smith, Arkansas, and we did love it there. The people were friendly and the pace was slow. Milder winters and longer gardening seasons were a lure for us as well, and so I agreed. "Let's do it!"

All our plans hinged on us selling our house quickly. We had a healthy amount in savings, which would tide us over until we could get settled in Arkansas, but there was not much wiggle room for a slow sale on our home.

But as the months went by, the money ran out.

We were maintaining our bills, but food was getting scarce. I was becoming confused. *Where is the new job You have lined up for us?* I asked, raising my eyes to Heaven. *I am ready, Lord. I am ready to sing Your praises when the blessings come! I am prepared!*

Still no one bought our house. Jay had travelled down to Arkansas to find a new place to live. We wanted land with the possibility of a large garden and maybe animals. A homestead. But what he found was a house on just under 2 acres in a lake community. There could be no animals, but at least there was land and the price was right.

We found a house in Arkansas, so where is the buyer of our current home? I wondered. I was getting anxious to move South, and even more anxious about our empty cupboards.

One day, as I was stressing about our dwindling finances and had nothing for dinner, I found myself on my knees. This sort of prayer was unusual for me, for it was an act of humility—a virtue of which, in the past, I had never thought I needed.

But there I was, finally asking Our Lord for His help. What I needed at that point was not a new job for Jay or a new, wonderful life for my family. I just needed dinner. *Please, Lord, show me how I am to care for my family. How do I give Jay the support he needs and the security and nourishment our children need to stay healthy? I cannot do this without You. Where are You?*

Pride had prevented us from letting our friends know how bad things truly were, so when the doorbell rang, I was surprised at the gift that awaited my family. It was one of our friends from church. "Hi Cassandra! I was just finishing up our Angel Food orders at church and realized we had an extra box no one had claimed. I thought I might bring it by to see if you had any use for it."

I was momentarily stunned. Then tears welled up in my eyes. *You have no idea.* "Thank you so much!" I gushed. "Yes, we can definitely use this food." *Oh sweet Consolation, how You fill my heart to bursting with love for You!*

A few anonymous donations of money arrived at our home over the next few weeks, helping us survive until we were ready to go, allowing me to comfortably place myself back into the hands of Our Lord. I was reassured that things may be a little rough, but He would always be with us, and I took comfort knowing we would continue to be taken care of. I was learning to trust in God, which was good. But at this point it was still on my terms.

Looking back at this time, I see how my previous life built on physical comfort and materialism was an obstacle for true growth. Never having been exposed to the lives of the Saints or a proper understanding of suffering, I thought that once I was converted I would be forever protected from misfortune. Or if I did suffer a cross, it would be minor and any temporal consolation I received would far outweigh the cross itself.

I was not alone in this error, as many friends of different religious backgrounds also believed in this false idea, a faith built on self instead of on God. Our rose-colored glasses prevented us from seeing the many varied ways Our Lord calls us to a deeper faith. When our flawed faith fails us, we are left with a sense of despair and an inability to see the greater love that lies beneath. It is only by responding to the grace of God that our hearts be opened and ready for the lessons we still must learn.

With our house still on the market, we made our move to the South. The owners of our new home were gracious enough to allow us to rent from them for a few months until we sold our old house, but by this time we were paying for two homes, and had no prospect of money coming in.

Thankfully our Chicago house sold a few months later and we no longer had to borrow from my sister to pay for that mortgage. Jay pounded the pavement, looking for any kind of work. We had some temporary relief from the sale of our home, which made me feel more confident that things were about to change for the better. I simply waited for the Good God to present us with His next gift.

It never came. At least not in the form I expected.

Instead of a wonderful new life in the South, full of happy homeschooling friends and affluent living, we were shunned by our neighbors for being Catholic and "joining forces with the Whore of Babylon." I had to defend the Catholic faith against the most bizarre accusations I had ever heard. Thankfully, with the help of a few apologetics books, my research further confirmed me in the Catholic faith, allowing me to see the errors in the questions posed to me. I am actually grateful for those who questioned my faith, for without their persistence, I never would have come to find the Truth.

We had recently shed the chains of credit card debt, but now had to return to them to pay our bills. We began the rapid descent towards bankruptcy. Once again that low lying, constant grumble in my stomach hinted at what our future might hold.

We were incredibly blessed to have found a treasure of a priest nearby, though, who helped usher my family to a different level of spirituality. Father M was a humble, holy priest who celebrated Mass with a level of reverence I had never before witnessed. Fellow parishioners considered him the Forrest Gump of priests, witnessing tremendous moments in foreign history, and knowing personally the kinds of people and world leaders one only reads about in the news. Yet, with his amazing past, here he was in a doublewide trailer-sized church in Nowhere, Arkansas.

Up until this time, we had only been to Masses that were uplifting and energizing. We had left those Masses feeling excited about being Catholic, but never really knowing what being Catholic actually meant.

Father's Masses, however, were different, and instead of leaving cheerful and energized, I left Mass in a meditative mood. A hunger was born in me, and for the first time in my life I realized there was far more to the Catholic faith than I had ever realized. As we slowly slipped back into poverty, my heart was being filled with riches.

During this time, an online friend of mine sent me two books that changed my life forever. The first book was *The Apostolate of Holy Motherhood*, and the other was St Louis de Montfort's *The Secret of the Rosary*.

I read the motherhood book first, in one sitting. I was riveted at what it contained, my eyes opened to what Our Lord and Our Lady were truly capable of. I had never heard of the kind of calling this book was challenging me to live and I was inspired to try to live a life for Christ instead of for myself.

Honestly, I only read the book once—the conversion it spurred in me was enough—and I cannot even recall what it was about that book that caused such a profound change in my outlook in life. Probably any book that explained in a little more detail about offering up our love and suffering to Our Lord through Our Lady would have done it for me. But after flourishing under the gentle care of Father M, I seemed to be ripe for change, and that book was the springboard I needed to take me to another level of love for Our Lord.

St. Louis de Montfort's book was also inspiring, but in a different way. While the first book suggested to me a better way to live, *The Secret of the Rosary* showed me a better way to pray. It wasn't even the entire book that did this, but rather a small section in the back, where the Saint outlined a specific way in which to pray the rosary.

His 'first method' as it is referred to in the book, calls us to ask for specific virtues as we pray each mystery. *That sounds interesting,* I thought. *I'll give it a try.*

"We offer you, Lord Jesus, this first decade in honor of your Incarnation. Through this mystery and the intercession of your holy Mother we ask for humility of heart."

Humility. Interesting. I had heard that the cornerstone of all virtues relied on a humble heart. Perhaps we just ask for this virtue first because we need it the most. And so I began to pray the prayers I already knew by heart, but concentrated on the mystery and virtue before me.

The Incarnation. Humility. God becoming man and subjecting Himself to the trials and tribulations of human life for love of us. Not as a fully grown man established in knowledge and power, but as a tiny baby housed within the womb of Mary.

Humility.

And then I took it a step further to the Annunciation. Mary alone with her prayer. An angel appears and completely changes the course of her entire life. She was greeted as only royalty was greeted: Hail Mary. No peasant was ever greeted with such an honorable address, and this greeting troubled her. And then the angel gives her a message. A request from God Almighty Himself, asking her to participate in His plan of salvation. This was not what she had been preparing for. It was not the life she had assumed she would lead. But she was always open to God's graces and had no will of her own but that of God's greater will for her life. No anger. No shock. An absolute fiat to God's will.

Humility.

What lessons is Mary teaching me within this mystery? When God has chosen me to be an instrument of His greater plan, how have I responded in the past? I was surprised to see that my first thoughts were always, "What is in it for me?" I felt that every time God made a change in my life, it should be for my further happiness and comfort in this world. This view was completely at odds with the lesson beneath the Incarnation and Annunciation. And all this came to me, just from my first time praying the first Joyful Mystery!

I finished the Glory Be and then prayed, "May the grace of the mystery of the Incarnation come into me and make me truly humble."

I had goosebumps. *What just happened?*

I prayed each of the 15 mysteries in this way, drawing from it whatever Our Lady wanted me to learn. It was as though centuries of wisdom was opened up to me, if only I was able to comprehend it all. I waited anxiously each night for the children and Jay to go to sleep so I could find time to spend at Our Lady's feet, taking in all she had to show me in the Gospel through her eyes. She demonstrated perfectly each virtue as it was illustrated in the appropriate mystery and my soul was enflamed with a love for Christ at last. Not for what He could do for me, for what He had already done. It was a love built on base gratitude, trampled pride, and a repentant heart. Another conversion.

Up to this point, I had probably prayed a total of two rosaries in my life. I didn't understand how it helped me grow in holiness and truly considered it vain repetition interspersed with a few hat tips to some Gospel stories. It made no sense to me and I thought anyone who gushed about how much they loved the rosary must be trying to lasso others into the unfortunate prayer trap into which they themselves had fallen. But now, the rosary became a prayer I craved, eager to continue the lessons I learned at Our Lady's feet.

At this time in our lives, we were on the verge of losing our home in Arkansas. The thought of becoming homeless had frightened me at first, but after many nights with Our Lady, I realized what I must do. It was a risk, I knew, but what if it actually worked? I took a deep breath, prayed about my special intention and opened myself up to God's will, while learning to let go of my own. In doing so, I completely changed my perspective and distanced myself from my family to grow closer to the Lord.

This was not an act of abandonment. On the contrary, this shift brought me closer to my children and husband than I ever was before.

My oldest daughter, Virginia, still recalls those days in Arkansas as some of her happiest memories.

"You do realize we were on the verge of losing our home, don't you?" I asked her.

She shook her head in amazement. "I never had a clue. All I remember was how wonderful it was to be home with you all the time and how happy we all were."

Indeed, Our Lord worked on my heart in powerful ways those stressful months. I had decided that I would no longer be a part of the problem, wringing my hands each day over the meager income Jay was able to scrape in for us. I was a child of God. And as such, I was placed within this family to perform a service both to Jay and his children, and to God Himself. *I am Yours, Lord. Do unto me according to Your word.*

I no longer worried about my own security and comfort. I just focused on keeping my family as comfortable and cheerful as possible. I imagined myself as a nun of sorts, praying for food each day, praying for the strength to persevere, praying for patience, and above all, praying to do His will, whatever it may be.

You, Lord, know my weaknesses far better than I. Please reveal to me what causes me to stumble, that I may one day be with You in Heaven. Not for my own glory or joy, Lord, but for Your greater glory. For truly, what greater glory can there be to Your credit than for my wretched soul to be saved?

If we lost our home and lived in a cardboard box, it was my duty to make sure they were as comfortable and well cared for as possible. I was no longer afraid. I simply strove to be the love my family needed. Be the love they will remember and draw from when times were hard and I was no longer around. Be the love Christ showed to us all as He gave His last drop of blood.

I looked to the Saints, my brothers and sisters who triumphed, and gleaned from them the lessons they taught. How to nurture a sacrificial heart. How to embrace poverty. How to remain cheerful in adversity. I concentrated on how fulfilling His will results in far more blessings than focusing on my will alone. For the first time in my life, I understood the sort of heart that was needed to gain a martyr's crown.

I absolutely desired that God's will be done over my own and prayed that if I misunderstood His will, He would know my heart and know my intention was as pure as my heart was capable.

While I had by no means reached anything close to a conquered will within me, my heart continued to strive towards perfecting my compass to always point wherever God wanted me to go.

I recalled my Confirmation Day, so many years before:

"I choose St. Theresa of Avila."

"And why do you choose her?" the bishop asked.

"Because I am always striving to be perfect!"

I was a fool then, convincing myself that my lust for physical and social perfection was a badge of virtue instead of the scarlet letter it truly was. Achieving such perfection was easy compared to what St. Matthew now called me to do: "Be you therefore perfect, as also your heavenly Father is perfect." (Matthew 5:48)

This call to perfection was not some special calling just for me. Nor was it a pious attempt to fill me with spiritual pride. Rather, this call to perfection is for all of God's children. Resigned to the humdrum life of a stay-at-home, homeschooling mother seemed like the perfect place to quietly work out my salvation with fear and trembling. I had already been tried by fire, or so I thought, and was now to be tried in patience, persevering through my daily life, finally setting aside my desire for leisurely lunches in a café or the quiet life of a hermit.

A few more weeks of close calls and several surprise boxes of food from Father M came and went, and we finally had to claim bankruptcy. It was another vicious blow to my pride, and another chance to trust in God's most terrifying yet soothing request: Accept *Thy will be done.*

Jay finally landed a steady job working for the local affiliate for a worldwide charity organization. We had a steady paycheck at last and prayed things would begin to be better for us all, but soon we faced the fact that even with his new steady employment, we could no longer afford our modest home.

During this time, we developed a strong desire to move to the country and wanted to try our hands at being semi-sufficient. I dreamed of raising gardens like my mother had when I was growing up. I imagined the romance of quieter times, making homemade butter in the kitchen while wondering little eyes watched in awe. I planned on canning our food and learning to make soap. I relished the vision of me gently shooing away chickens as I hitched my long calico skirt above my ankles, off to collect eggs in the nest boxes and pick a few daisies on my way back into the house. Our garden would offer us an endless bountiful harvest of fresh, organic produce, and I imagined more than a few wild antics involving my sweet children and handfuls of straw and maybe an earthworm or two. I would always cook all my meals from scratch, wash the dishes by hand, and hang the laundry out to dry. I would lovingly sew skirts for my girls and myself until the wee hours of the morning, hopefully with the help of a few forest critters and a bluebird. Oh yeah. And of course, only bake whole wheat bread using freshly hand-ground organic wheat berries.

"Are you going to grow your own wheat, too?" my mother asked me one day, exasperated with my vision.

"Of course not!" I replied. "Who has time for wheat fields?" *I mean really.*

Then, one day, rays of heavenly sunshine shone upon a worn down, one story house on nine acres of rocks and weeds, and we decided that this humble Oklahoma property was to be our home. Jay could still commute to his job each day, while I got to play Little House on the Prairie with my growing brood.

I dreamt many dreams of cozy country living, and while some dreams have been realized, I have by no means been able to claim I have perfected the Little House on the Prairie life I had envisioned. Yes, I learned how to make homemade soap, sewed clothes for my daughters and myself, canned our own produce and chicken meat, and filled my home with the aroma of freshly baked whole wheat bread. But while these are among my favorite homesteading activities, I have also been spotted purchasing loaves of Wonderbread more often than my pride likes to admit. And sometimes I even buy our skirts. Premade. From Walmart.

It has been said that a garden's best fertilizer is the farmer's shadow, however I discovered the alarming fact that my shadow served to be more of a deadly dose of Round-Up for my plants. So I humbly turned over the gardening to my mother and oldest daughter.

While I found great satisfaction in washing our laundry by hand, most of our laundry would be done the modern way. Roosters terrified me, goats escaped almost daily, the weather was frightening, and chigger bites have proved themselves to be a surprisingly effective source of sanctification for us all.

Indeed, most of my silly notions of living the good life were buried in the compost pile early on in our adventure. But we found a balance that worked well for our family and we did not regret the changes we made. It was by no means a glamorous life, but it was our life, and I chose to live it as well as I could. Resigned to this quiet existence, I continued to grow in my faith and trust in my Lord, wanting nothing more than to be able to turn over my will to Him without reserve. A complete resignation to my own will, that God's will be done.

Little did I know how strongly that was to be put to the test.

***

Take, Lord, and receive all my liberty, my memory, my understanding, and my entire will, all I have and call my own. You have given all to me. To you, Lord, I return it. Everything is yours; do with it what you will. Give me only your love and your grace, that is enough for me. Amen.

—St. Ignatius of Loyola

CHAPTER 7

"In suffering, love, and in loving, suffer!"
—Blessed Maria Lopez of Jesus

"Cassandra, your father has esophageal cancer," my mother announced one September evening. "He has only a few months to live."

A rush of emotions and disbelief came over me. *Dad has cancer?*

Memories of the man I adored throughout childhood came to me, as if preparing me for all I was about to lose. The six-mile-long Saturday morning bike rides to a neighboring town, stopping for a root beer in the café, and riding back home. The hours-long Wagner opera marathons, discovering the secret stories written within the music. Listening to Tolkein's tales come to life through his expressive, baritone voice. Umpire at my softball games. And a loving provider and protector to us all. *Cancer? There is so much more I need to learn from him!*

We arranged for the whole family to travel to Michigan to spend time with him while he was still able to communicate. I spent most of our trip North remaining cheerful for my children, but praying nonstop within my heart. *A miracle, oh Lord, is not beyond Your capabilities. But if it be Your will that my father dies, show me what You would have me do.*

Those first two weeks were joyful times, listening to many stories we had never heard before, enjoying a few Wagnerian opera fests and simply basking in the light his life still shone forth. We celebrated Thanksgiving several weeks early, knowing that as time progressed eating would become more difficult and we would not have the energy or even desire to acknowledge the holiday as we should.

It soon became apparent that my mother, whose own health was failing, could not care for my father alone. So after my sisters' families came and went, Ryan and I remained behind to assist wherever we could. Fulton was only a few months old at this time, so he stayed with me as well.

In my pride, I had plans. Plans to pray with my father, read the writings of the Saints to him, to go through the daily Mass readings and meditations in my *Magnificat* subscription. I wanted to show my father the beauty of the rosary and how the virtues within those Mysteries could help him. I desired nothing more than for him to obtain the great grace of perfect contrition for his sins, allowing him entrance into Heaven for all eternity. I prayed for a happy, holy death for him, surrounded by the Sacraments and priestly prayers. And I prayed for strength, for myself and for my mother, that we would be capable of ministering to him in any way he needed.

However, I was completely unprepared for the level of suffering I would witness. And I failed.

My father's cancer moved from his esophagus to his stomach and soon he was only able to take in liquids. He decided against any treatments and refused to go into the hospital or into a hospice center. He wanted to die at home, on his favorite couch, with his music surrounding him at all times. We employed a caretaker through a home hospice center who visited us several times a week, guiding us on how to best tend to his needs and preparing us for what was to come.

His last few weeks were painful to watch and I will admit I was not as much of a help as I wanted to be. I had never been faced with such raw suffering before and felt completely helpless in its grip. Soon, even swallowing his liquids became too painful, and medics from the hospice center came to take him to the hospital where they would give him a feeding tube. As the van pulled out of the driveway, I cried and prayed like never before, hoping the surgery would be a success yet knowing I was going to lose my father soon.

Hours later, they returned, my father exhausted. The hospice medics wheeled him to his couch and made him as comfortable as they could, and then quietly left. My mother was in tears. "They couldn't give him a feeding tube. He has no stomach . . ."

His cancer, diagnosed only a few weeks earlier, had taken over his body so rapidly, there was no longer enough stomach left to take the feeding tube. He had left that morning fairly hopeful, thinking he would have maybe a few more weeks to live, and came home knowing now it would only be a matter of days.

Organ failure soon set in, requiring a doctor to come in on a regular basis to drain the fluid that rapidly collected in his abdomen, and his agony began. My parents' parish priest came to hear his final confession and receive the Eucharist, but I worried that his soul might slip into despair after he received the Sacraments. I wrestled nightly with an unseen force, fighting off my own despair while offering up whatever I could to protect him from the same demons that were haunting me.

Saddened that no priest could be with him when his last agony came, I directed my prayers towards my father obtaining perfect contrition and perseverance. I meditated constantly on the Sorrowful Mysteries, praying his suffering would help bring about his redemption. *May he suffer well, Lord. For his own salvation and for Your glory.* I prayed the rosary out loud for him. He held his beads and I prayed. He was always pensive during the Sorrowful Mysteries and I think Our Lord was doing His work on his heart.

I was truly beside myself for him, praying for God's mercy, and trying to overcome the last of my own aversion to suffering. Esophageal and stomach cancer does not let its victim go peacefully. And while my father was indeed spared much of the pain we were told to expect, the suffering was still immense. I tended to his physical needs, provided him with comfort as I could. Sometimes I read to him, other times I simply sat with him and held his hand in silence.

I called upon Our Lady to teach me to see Our Lord in my father, suffering his Passion, and forced myself to stay at his side, lovingly stroking his head on my lap or wiping vomit from his beard when my natural inclination was to run away. I recalled the days in Arkansas when I separated my heart from my will, denying my will for the sake of serving those I loved. There was no comparison between the financial worries I buffered from my children and the physical and spiritual suffering I tried to soothe for my father. But the servant's heart fought to reign supreme and I overcame my will for a time.

Around Thanksgiving, our family returned, and my father slowly withdrew within himself. He no longer communicated with us, but we never left his side. Lying down was too uncomfortable for him, so his last few days he remained sitting up, with his forehead resting on a pillow upon the hospital tray we set before him.

About three days before he passed, his sisters, my family and my sisters' families were all gathered around him. His head was resting on the table as usual and I was standing in front of him, leading everyone in prayer. Suddenly, he lifted his head, gazed at each one of us with clear eyes and said, "I love all of you so very much." He slowly put his head back down, and those were the last words we ever heard him utter.

Sweet Jesus, see the love. Take him home.

Those few precious weeks in Michigan were both beautiful and terrifying. I learned how precious and fragile life truly is and how much we need to rely on God to see us through. And I saw how one can freely choose to accept or resist the trials which God places before us.

Jay and I had fought for our marriage and won. We battled through poverty and learned to trust in God's goodness. And we survived those two months apart as my father died, under extremely stressful conditions, learning the value of sacrifice for love of family and the greater glory of God. But my personal lesson I learned through it all was the incredible love that is shown to us through suffering, and I thanked God for yet another lesson hard learned for the betterment of my soul.

I saw clearly for the first time how each cross with which I was blessed was fertile ground for conversion in my heart. Had I given up on Jay in the beginning, I never would have learned to accept my own wretchedness and learned to forgive, and I would not have turned to the Catholic faith. And had I given up or added to the panic surrounding our dire financial situation, I never would have purged myself of the grip materialism held upon my heart and learned to trust in God for all I needed, be grateful for all He has given and thankful for what He has taken. Nor would I have been inspired to nurture a servant's heart. And finally I was honored to behold the final work of sanctification, assisting another soul through suffering and helping usher my father to eternity, teaching me the invaluable lesson on how to truly love.

What now, Lord? I prayed.

The word 'prepare' came back to me one night, after tucking my children into bed and praying. Only this time, I did not casually brush it aside to simply wait for blessings. Nor did I overanalyze it, getting in a panic over a multitude of bad things that could happen. Instead, I understood for the first time that the call to prepare was an invitation to remain open to God's will in my life, no matter what He may bring. It was a gentle urging from Our Lord to nudge me forward, closer to becoming who He wanted me to become, and a suggestion that I remain close to His side, continuing to grow in faith, hope, and charity, while waiting for the next cross to come.

***

I thank You, Lord, for showing me both the beauty of life and the sorrow of death, so intricately woven throughout my father's last weeks. I thank You for the time we had together, for the lessons learned and the love revealed. Have mercy upon his soul, and bring him to Your Heavenly home. And have mercy on us all, that we live out our remaining years for Your glory, and please bless us with the grace of a holy death. Amen.

CHAPTER 8

"My hope is in Christ, who strengthens the weakest by His Divine help. I can do all in Him who strengthens me. His Power is infinite, and if I lean on him, it will be mine. His Wisdom is infinite, and if I look to Him for counsel, I shall not be deceived. His Goodness is infinite, and if my trust is stayed in Him, I shall not be abandoned."
—*St. Pope Pius X*

With my conversion to the Catholic faith came a deeper understanding of what it means to love and be loved. I was drawn to the Church's teachings of perfect contrition and longed for a soul perfectly united to His will through a perfect love for Him. I prayed for this great grace often—that I no longer felt sorrow for my sins because I feared His just punishments, but more so because they offend my God who is all good and deserving of all my love.

Never was I more sure that I received a small portion of this great grace than on that cold January day. I felt as though I should be in a rage or panic over Fulton's plight, and yet all I could think about was giving God glory through this affliction. I accepted it with humility, praying I was not just in a state of shock. "Maybe the gravity of this situation will hit me later," I reasoned. But I accepted the peace I felt at the time as a blessing and focused on what was to come.

The helicopter waited in the grassy field behind the tiny elementary school. As soon as we arrived, they began readying my son for transport. One of the air medics introduced herself to me and explained, "We are going to take Fulton to Hillcrest Hospital in Tulsa. They have an excellent burn unit there and they will take good care of your son. Do you have a way of getting to Tulsa?"

"I will be there," I numbly replied. Tulsa was about two hours from where we lived and the thought of being so far from Fulton for so long was agonizing. *Dear Lord, there has to be another way.*

"I just wanted to make sure you knew where you had to go, because unfortunately we cannot take you there ourselves. Only patients can ride with us. Pilot's rules." I nodded, resigned to whatever was to happen. She left me sitting on the step of the ambulance while they continued to work on Fulton from within.

Ryan arrived right behind us and we sat for a time in silent shock. My oldest son, aspiring to be a first responder in the Air Force, was not present when the explosion occurred. I had just sent him three miles down the road to the gas station to pick up another bag of ice, just in case we needed it, and by the time he returned, the first responders were already at our home. His heart must have been divided, wanting to use the medical knowledge he was learning, yet unable to offer any assistance.

So he comforted me instead. Few words came to us, but just having his strong presence with me helped ease my pain. I silently pleaded with Our Lord, and thanked Him, all at the same time. Pleading that Fulton's life be spared, if it be His holy will. And thanking Him for the first responders, my family, the air medics, and for the time I was given to have Fulton in my life—my heart overflowed with gratefulness and yet such sorrow at the same time. A bittersweet contradiction that only made sense through the light of a love for God.

I walked to the other side of the ambulance and caught sight of the pilot. He stood, still and silent, at the door of the vehicle, dark slacks and a jacket, and a pair of shades. He reminded me of my father, so much so I stared for a moment in disbelief. This man resembled my father, not as he struggled in his final stages of cancer, but as the strong, kind man I always knew. *Dad, if you are somewhere where you can hear me, please help me get to Tulsa. Do not let me be separated from my son.* I then prayed for the repose of my father's soul and trusted Our Lord knew better than I how this day should end.

I returned to the ambulance step I was sitting on before and focused completely on emptying myself of anxiety. *Thy will be done, Lord. I reserve nothing for myself. Even if you are to take Fulton from me, Thy will be done.*

A few minutes passed, then the medic again approached me, looking a little confused. "How much do you weigh?" she asked.

Unsure why she was asking me, I felt that now was not the time to be shy. A lot was riding on the truthfulness of my answer, I felt, and so I answered, "About 155." She nodded and disappeared.

Moments later she returned to me, this time with a smile on her face. "I can't believe this is happening!" she exclaimed. "The pilot says you may fly with us!" *Praise God!* That last wave of relief cleansed me of any temporal anxiety. *Thank you, Lord!* "You have no idea how huge this is. He has never done this before. Ever!"

She had every reason to be in complete awe at what was about to happen. Three years after Fulton's accident, Jay had a chance meeting with the pilot at the Clear Creek Abbey's annual work day. The men recalled that dreadful day, and after discussing his usual 'no fly' rule, Jay asked why he consented to me flying with them. He shook his head and said, "I have no idea. For some reason I was just compelled to let her come with." Praise God for moving this good man's heart.

They finally stabilized Fulton enough to load him into the helicopter, and as soon as he was safely strapped in, they began showing me where I was to sit and what not to do while flying. The list was long, and a little unnerving. It was a tight fit for us all, and my shoulder brushed dangerously close to the door more times than I was comfortable with. But I was going to be able to stay with Fulton. And that was all that mattered.

I was given a set of headphones to protect my ears, and if anything needed to be conveyed to me, they would switch my headset on and speak to me. I nodded to indicate I understood all of the safety rules and settled myself for the 28-minute flight. 28 minutes. Just enough time to pray the Joyful Mysteries of the rosary.

I prayed out loud as we flew, figuring the helicopter was far too noisy for anyone but Our Lord and Our Lady to hear me.

The Annunciation for humility—*I give You, Lord, my fiat and surrender my will, that it be perfectly conformed to Yours. Strengthen me in my weakness, that I do not rebel against this cross. Help me to see Your greater plan in this, and help me trust that this is to be our path to salvation. Let it be done unto us according to Your word.*

The Visitation for charity towards our neighbor—*Mary came to St. Elizabeth to tend to her temporal needs. But her greatest, most charitable gift was bringing You to her. Please remind me to be grateful for all acts of love offered to us along the way, and to remain attentive to any souls You send our way to help them through their own trials and bring to them Your Light.*

The Nativity for a spirit of poverty—*I am headed far from home. I must trust in You to see to it that all of our basic needs are to be met. Just as Mary and Joseph had to huddle in a stable, they cared not for worldly needs, for they had the Infant Jesus in their arms. We too will be far from home, but as long as I keep You close to my heart, You will provide for whatever our needs might be. And whatever I may lack, I know You withhold it from me for my own benefit.*

The Presentation for wisdom and purity—*please bless me with the grace of wisdom, to think clearly and make the right decisions for my son. Protect me from the temptation to indulge myself in pity. And keep me pure of heart and purpose, allowing no selfishness to enter.*

And finally, the Finding in the Temple to convert my heart, amend my life and for those who are lost to the Catholic faith—*may this cross refine my soul as You see fit, O Lord, and if it be Your will, may I find ways to quietly share my faith with those I meet who may be suffering from darkness.*

The flight was fairly uneventful, and I do not recall much of the sights below. All of my attention was focused on prayer and what the other medic was doing to Fulton. A few times he had to make some quick adjustments or inject something into his IV, either for pain, anxiety or 'stabilization.'

I finished my rosary a few minutes before we landed, and the speakers in my headset turned on. "We are about to land. Do not open your door until we say it is safe," the female medic said. I nodded my head. "And thank you for your prayers. We all certainly need them!" I smiled. I still do not know if my microphone was on the entire time or not, but at least I know my prayers touched another heart that day.

They unloaded Fulton, and we quickly followed suit, ducking beneath the propellers as we ran towards the door. The hospital roof was wet with drizzle, and I had pulled my sweater tightly around me as we entered the hospital. Very little was said to me—the air medics relayed Fulton's status to the nurses as we sped to the emergency room. They had cleared a room for him earlier, and were waiting for his arrival.

We were separated at the door to his room. Fulton was to be attended to by the doctors and the holy angels that my friends and family were already sending, and I was ushered to a private consultation room. It was a small square room, able to seat about five people with a coffee table in the center. A few well-read magazines failed to distract me, so I sat and simply stared at my hands.

I didn't want to call Jay quite yet, fearing I would be on the phone when a doctor came in. And after about 10 minutes, a woman entered the room. There was some paperwork to fill out while I answered the more important questions verbally so the information could be quickly relayed to the doctors. Then, "We have an excellent burn unit here, Mrs. Poppe," I was reassured with a smile. "A doctor will be in with you shortly."

At that point, I decided it was safe to call Jay. "We're in Tulsa," I told him. Knowing he would want to hear about Fulton before talking about himself, I told him what I knew—which was pretty much nothing. "They tell me they have a very good burn unit here, so I am comfortable with this. I haven't seen Fulton since they took him, and I haven't spoken to a doctor yet. It took them awhile to get him stable and he does not seem to be aware of what is going on at this point. They will fill me in as soon as they are through examining him and I will be allowed in his room after that. How are you?"

Jay's eyebrows and hair were singed. And thanks to the heavy layers of clothing, Jay only sustained second degree burns on his hands and inner forearms due to putting Fulton's fire out. The emergency room personnel, hearing of our tragic plight, moved Jay up to the front of the line, making it a priority to get Jay treated and sent home as soon as possible, in case Fulton did not survive the night.

Jay was very reluctant to talk about himself at all and kept redirecting his questions to Fulton's status. Finally, we wrapped up our phone call. "Please call Father A," I begged. "Fulton needs an anointing." As soon as he could, he assured me, he would call the local FSSP priest. We tearfully said our goodbyes and I resumed waiting.

For some reason the consultation room seemed too quiet. Too small. I was unable to pray, save for a few short words here and there. I suppose I was just waiting for something new, something more concrete to pray about. Then, there was a knock at the door, and a tall slender man with glasses and a young, friendly face entered the room.

The doctor introduced himself. He extended his hand to me, which I took for a moment while I waited to hear the news. His expression was grave. "I am so very sorry for what happened to your son."

"Thank you, Doctor," a lump was swelling, burning in my throat. I knew what he was going to tell me was not going to be good.

He paused a moment, as if considering how he should break the news. "We are unable to admit Fulton to our burn unit. He cannot stay here."

The most illogical thoughts began running through my mind. *So what now? Do we take him home? How do we get him to another hospital? What does this even mean?* Visions of me rushing Fulton to another hospital in a taxi cab distracted me from what the doctor told me next. "Burn injuries are unlike other injuries, and while we have an excellent burn unit here, due to his age and the level of his burns, we cannot give him the kind of care he requires. We have made some phone calls and think we have found you some help. Have you heard of the Shriners?"

Of course. My eight year old girl's memory came to me of four or five men in matching jackets and tasseled red fez hats riding their flying carpet vehicles in crazy circles in the Harvard, Illinois Milk Day Parade. "Who are they?" I had asked my father.

"Shriners," he answered. "They have hospitals for children."

And that was pretty much my experience with the Shriners. *OK then. Flying carpets instead of taxis . . .*

"They have a few hospitals across the country that specialize in children's burns. Truly, your son's best chances are with them. Two representatives are on their way here to talk to you about what they are able to do."

I was still reeling. I had settled in my mind that Hillcrest had the best possible care, and hearing that these experts were unable to do anything for Fulton shook me up. *How bad was he?* My heart cried out to Jay, fearful I would be asked to make decisions without his counsel. *Lord, please give me wisdom and the ability to discern. Things are happening too fast.*

"We estimate that Fulton has severe burns on about 50% of his body and first degree burns all over. We have him sedated and on IVs. He is sweating and urinating which is really good news. Do you remember the last time he ate?"

"Umm . . . About 8:30 this morning. Waffles." The scent of peanut butter and maple syrup came to me. And then gasoline and burnt flesh.

"His bowels sound OK right now, too. We will watch that. But our main concern is swelling. We did a basic assessment of his airways and do not see too much damage, but swelling could still close his airway off. We are prepared for that as well." And so went his assessment. I do not remember the details he told me that day. It was too much to take in. Worry and then relief kept taking the upper hand with my emotions as he ticked off each injury and prognosis.

Then finally, mercifully, "Would you like to see him?" He escorted me to his room, the rest of the staff strangely silent as I passed them in the hallway.

When I first saw him, I was surprised at what I found. For some reason I expected him to look more like a patient and less like a fresh victim. *Shouldn't they have cleaned up his wounds? And wrapped him in bandages?* The tiny patches of good skin on his face still had soot and pieces of burnt hair stuck to it. In fact, in the harsh hospital light, he looked even dirtier than what I remembered. His face was beginning to swell, and with most of his bone structure obscured by the disfiguring injuries, he was almost unrecognizable.

His entire body was covered with a sheet, except for his left foot which stuck out to the side and slightly off the bed. Just like always. Jay called that his sleep snorkel—that one foot free of all covers at night as he slept, no matter how cold the house was. My grandmother slept like that, and I am told I sleep like that as well. I almost smiled. His face was too wretched to look at. But I had his foot. His perfect little foot, dirty toes and all. "May I touch his foot?" I asked, fearful of infection or of hurting him.

"Of course," the doctor answered. "I will leave you with him, but if you have any questions I will remain close by." A ham sandwich, chips, and a Sprite were brought to me, and a nurse stayed near us, but was silent.

I stroked his foot and told him I was with him. "Mama is holding your foot, Fulton. Can you feel me?" There was no response. "You are being so very brave. I am so proud of you. I love you so, so much, Buddy!" My words were scarcely above a whisper, afraid that any noise might cause him distress. I simply wanted peace for him, in whatever form I could provide. *But please Lord*, I prayed, *let Father A get here soon!*

After talking with the doctor, I was now armed with a new list of prayer requests. So, I got to work. *Keep his airway open. No infection. Heal Jay so he can meet us wherever the Shriners will be taking us. Keep me strong. Save my son. Thy will be done.*

Jim and Gary, two representatives of the Shriner's lodge that would sponsor Fulton's care, soon arrived. I left Fulton's side to discuss our next steps. They were two friendly, middle-aged gentlemen with true hearts for Fulton's plight, and I was thankful to be able to discuss a plan of action for Fulton. Before long, everything was laid out for me, and I recalled the reassurances I felt as I prayed the Nativity earlier that day, for a spirit of poverty and for humility to accept any help offered to us.

They explained that Hillcrest Hospital would release Fulton to their care. They had already arranged for medical transport. A Lear jet would fly us to Galveston where Fulton would receive the best care available worldwide. Shriners would provide a place for me to stay. They would feed me. They would even clothe me, if needed. And they would cover any medical expenses the hospital incurred that our insurance did not cover.

The jet was already on its way. The only possible problem we had was the weather. There were storms between Tulsa and Galveston, and if the pilot was not comfortable with the trip to Texas, we would go to Cleveland instead. Or perhaps Galveston, or Cleveland. It made minimal difference to me except for the fact that Texas was only about 600 miles from home and Cleveland was quite a bit more.

I finally decided Galveston would be better overall, so I asked St. Scholastica to help us. *You obtained from Our Lord a drastic change in weather before. Please, intercede for me and ask Him to do it again!* Needless to say, the bad weather dissipated and we prepared to head to Galveston.

At one point, while we waited for the jet to arrive at the airport, Fulton crashed. I do not know what exactly happened, but Jim calmly talked to me in the hallway while the doctors and nurses frantically worked on my son. He reassured me that they were top-notch caregivers at Hillcrest and they would not release Fulton unless they were sure he would survive the flight. Forced to face the fact that Fulton may indeed die, I tried to focus on what time I would still have with my son. *Please Lord, if it be Your will that he not survive, I beg You to have mercy on him and take Him into Your loving arms. Tell him I love Him and to pray for us.*

Evening came, and they finally had Fulton stabilized when the jet landed in Tulsa. No one told me at the time where the jet came from, but a year later one of the Shriners' nurses explained to Jay that most jets that fly the patients into Galveston belonged to businessmen—usually 'big oil' executives who donate the use of their planes to get children such as Fulton to whichever hospital their injuries demanded. I am so grateful to the anonymous person who was so willing to share his treasures in such a meaningful way.

As soon as Fulton was ready, we took an ambulance to the airport. I sat in the front with the ambulance driver. "Would you like my dinner?" He offered me the contents of his brown paper lunch bag. "Truly, I am not hungry. And you have a long night ahead of you yet." Though I was touched by the constant care I was receiving that day from so many strangers, I gratefully declined.

The evening was gray and wet, the rain continuing to fall and I allowed myself to appreciate the beauty of the raindrops as they slithered down the windshield. Soothing waters. Tears from Heaven. A moment's rest and mental respite before diving down again into the drama that was still unfolding.

Soon we arrived where the jet awaited. I was surprised at how small it was and wondered how we were all going to fit. A gentleman in a dark suit and long black raincoat stood by the jet. One of the medics steered me towards him, saying, "He has an umbrella for you—we have to get the plane ready before we get in." This silent, well-dressed individual exuded peace and comfort to me. I had no idea who he was, but if I had to compare what standing next to a Guardian Angel must be like, it would be as it was with him. When it was time for me to board the jet, I thanked him for the shelter he offered. He nodded and said, "I'm so sorry," and that was all we ever said.

The jet was surprisingly spacious on the inside. There were two pilots in front, separated from us by a partial wall and open doorway. Fulton was strapped in first, his entire stretcher secured in place where passenger seats would have been placed. Behind his stretcher and across the aisle were the seats for the medics. I was seated in the back, directly in front of the baggage area. There was a complimentary bottle of water and a fancy, full-color brochure about the plane. If it were not for the still unfamiliar olfactory mixture of medicine and burned flesh, I would have thought I was about to fly towards some tropical paradise.

The medical flight crew was cheerful, and the two pilots, two medics, Fulton and I were soon in the air. Being told it would be about a 45-minute flight, I began an entire rosary of all 15 mysteries. The Joyful Mysteries were as they were before, confirming for me what my path should be.

As I began the Sorrowful Mysteries, I gazed out the window. The rain clouds spread out beneath us like a thick, dark, misty sea, but the sunset was brilliant. The sun, it appeared, was being swallowed up by black, and my heart cried out to it as the final sliver of light sank beneath the rain clouds. *Don't leave me, Lord*, I prayed. And the light disappeared, still shining beneath those storm clouds for others, but the light felt lost to me. *So be it.*

Hail Mary, full of grace.

"Fulton is awake," one of the medics interrupted. "Why don't you let him know you are here."

"Hi Fulton!" I called from my seat, "You are being so brave! I am riding here with you and I will always be with you, OK?" His hand moved a little and the medic smiled. "I love you, Buddy!"

"That's right, Buddy! Your mom is here and you are flying in a jet. Have you ever flown in a jet before?" A slight shake of his head. "Well, now you can tell all your girlfriends that you have flown in a Lear jet. We are going so fast! About 635 miles an hour! Isn't that cool?" A faint nodded. The medic looked up at me and grinned. "He's going to be fine!" he beamed.

That brief moment was the last time Fulton responded to any stimulation for days, and I treasured the memory of those few seconds, hoping those would not be his last. Throughout the rest of the flight, they administered various injections into his IV line or pumped oxygen into his lungs. His face continued to swell and its texture was horrifying to behold.

I closed my eyes and continued my rosary. *Mother of God, please show me what I am to learn and strengthen me as I join you on this journey.*

The Agony in the Garden for obedience and perfect contrition—*once again I pray above all things that Thy will be done. Please prepare me to be willingly obedient to Your will no matter what, all for the love of You. I shall use this cross as a necessary remedy for my wayward heart and ask forgiveness for the sins I have committed that made Your Passion necessary.*

The Scourging at the Pillar for a spirit of mortification—*Help me, Lord Jesus, to help my son suffer for love of You. And Mother Mary, help me to offer the suffering I will endure as I helplessly watch my child struggle. May our sufferings be bound in love for all those in need of prayers and especially for my friends and loved ones who are suffering their own crosses.*

The Crowning with Thorns for contempt of this world— *Please keep me focused on the spiritual battles more so than the physical battles we may face. May all triumphs be for God's glory and may I keep none for myself. And should Fulton die, may I rejoice in the Heavenly crown he may gain, which will have no thorns of pride, false grandeur, or bitterness. And I ask that the same grace be preserved for me.*

The Carrying of the Cross for patience—*Yes, Lord, please. They say we may be in Galveston for several months. Months. I grow weary so easily, Lord. Send me a Saint Veronica. Send me a Simon. And give to me this grace of patience as we travel this unknown road. I do not know what lies ahead, but I know the terrain will be brutal, even if I cannot yet see the details.*

The Crucifixion for a love of the Cross, a hatred of sin and the grace of a holy death for ourselves, our loved ones, and for all those in their last agony—*Mary, as you clung to the foot of your Son's Cross, please help me as I cling to Fulton's. Be my guide. Show me how to love that which causes unspeakable suffering. Show me how to comfort both my son and my Lord. And may all I offer up through this trial be for the salvation of our souls and for the final grace of true repentance and love of God for all the souls about to face Judgment.*

Indeed this journey will be mostly that of sorrow. And I was prepared.

I prayed the Glorious Mysteries next, assured that no matter what the outcome would be, God would be glorified.

The Resurrection for faith—*I believe, God, that You do all things out of love for us. May Your glorious Resurrection be a reminder to me that our ultimate goal is not a healing of body, but a healing of soul, and that the work being done in Fulton's tomb will one day bring You glory once the stone has been rolled away and Your works revealed. Only You know the final outcome. Help me have faith that "Thy will be done" should be done, and all will be well. And increase in my family the faith they will need as we stumble with this cross. Show us Your mercy and remind us You are God.*

The Ascension for hope—*Give me hope, Lord, that one day we shall follow You in Your Heavenly ascent. I will hope for Fulton's recovery, but as Saint Louis' mother once prayed, if you see in his future anything that keeps him from enjoying eternity with You, my greatest hope lies in You taking him to you now before that great separation should occur. The torments of Fulton's earthly suffering are slight compared to an eternal separation from You.*

The Descent of the Holy Ghost that I may know and love my faith, and share it with others—*How many souls, Lord, do you want us to touch? Will it be the souls of my family, that we strengthen each other in our faith? Or shall Fulton be a tool for a greater cause, still yet to be revealed? Give to me a greater understanding of my faith, especially what it means to suffer, and help me share this with those You place in my path.*

And do the same for Fulton, who will be your special messenger, should You choose to use him. Transform the injurious, disfiguring flames that consumed my son into a healing light for others. Thy will be done, Lord. Just show me what to do.

The Immaculate Conception and Mary's Assumption into Heaven for true devotion to her—*Thank you, Lord, for giving to us Your mother as our own. As such, may she bring me much comfort and motherly guidance over the next few months. May she continue to draw me closer to You. And may she be the mother to Fulton and to all my children when my own mothering abilities fall short.*

The Coronation, to persevere in the faith, to continue to grow in virtue, and to ultimately gain our own crowns in Heaven—*To be perfect as our Heavenly Father is perfect is a lifelong quest. Strengthen me on this journey, that this extra burden You have blessed us with will strengthen my soul rather than weaken it, and may it become a source of sanctification for my entire family. At every moment, we will be given a choice to nurture our pride or to grow in virtue; may I always choose those virtuous gems for my Heavenly crown.*

With the speed of an angel's wings, we arrived in Galveston in just short of an hour. Armed with a full rosary, I watched as the medics loaded Fulton's stretcher into the Shriner's van. He no longer resembled my beloved son at all, and only grave, hushed tones were used. Fear grew in the darkness, seeming to attach itself to the dampness that hung heavily in the air, seeping through the threads of my clothes, causing me to shiver.

Somberly, silently, I followed the stretcher. I craved at once both warmth and consolation. Though I was surrounded by medical staff, I suddenly felt alone. I followed them in the elevator and down the hallway like a lost child helpless to find her own way and forced to place all her trust in complete strangers. With no time for a last goodbye, I was escorted to the intensive care unit lobby on the second floor while Fulton was whisked into the waiting operating room.

The ICU lobby was quiet. It must have been after 9 p.m., as only a few nightlights were on. One entire wall, facing the UTMB Hospital across the street, was a wall of windows spanning the second and third floor. The third floor balcony looked down to where I was sitting, and the only sound I heard was the night custodian vacuuming the carpet on the floor above—a familiar, comforting sound. I closed my eyes and settled back onto the couch.

Soon, a woman came to me, offering me juice and a folder containing important information about the hospital and the kind of care Fulton would receive. I devoured both as she explained how the rest of the evening would go. The doctors would finish their evaluation and Fulton would get settled into his room. When I was comfortable leaving, one of the security guards would drive me to a furnished apartment where I could get some rest. They would then pick me up at around 7 a.m., and then the real work would begin. "There is a woman waiting for you downstairs. She says a common friend sent her. Shall I send her up?"

The woman, it turned out, was a regular reader of CatholicMom.com and the first angel I met in Galveston. The internet proved to be a lifeline for me during our trial, delivering prayers, friendship, and support in ways I never imagined.

Soon after I had left our house, my daughter Virginia hit my Facebook page with a plea for prayers. News spread like wildfire, and by the time we landed in Galveston, we had thousands praying for Fulton, from the elderly couple living next door, to a convent of nuns in Spain, another in Italy, and the nuns and monks at our own beloved Clear Creek Abbey. Over the next few months I would learn of the many prayer groups and religious orders in Germany, Bosnia, England, Australia, Ireland, and Canada as well as the multitudes of Masses and rosaries offered up for Fulton throughout the United States. And Lisa Hendey of

CatholicMom.com helped spread the word and gained for us not only powerful prayers to see us through, but rallied many people to donate to the fundraiser we needed to put in place to cover our quickly mounting expenses.

It was not just the Catholic community that banned together either. That same day, and many months thereafter, there was an ecumenical outpouring of charity and prayers sent Heavenward for our little boy. The most striking example, of course, is the deep dedication of the Bedouin Shrine in Muskogee, OK. Their tireless concern and financial backing of all his care has literally saved Fulton's life. We are profoundly grateful and consider it an honor to pray for them daily. In addition, the Baptist church down the road from us held a fundraising auction. Heritage Methodist Church in Van Buren, Arkansas, kept close tabs on Fulton's progress and continue to pray for him to this day. My sister-in-law, Kathy, and friends at St. Boniface Church in Fort Smith, Arkansas helped organize a wonderful musical fundraiser and all food was generously donated by a gourmet chef and her staff. My college roommate's church in Illinois, a junior high classroom in Wisconsin, multitudes of children from all over the country sent Fulton cards and little distractions. We were overwhelmed by the generosity and love that was showered upon us during this time and even to this day. Our Lord certainly allows us to be tried by fire, but at the same time relieves us in a multitude of little ways, that we not lose hope.

This first woman who reached out to me represented the countless souls who were touched by Fulton's accident and I was so grateful. She, a complete stranger to me, offered me companionship that first night, and let herself be available to me whenever I needed her. She took me to Mass that first Sunday, picked up and dropped off my mother at the airport later that month when she came to visit, and truly helped ease my burden.

As each minute passed, exhaustion began to take its toll and I lost all track of time. Thirty minutes or three hours later, a doctor appeared, still dressed in his mask and scrubs and gave me his initial assessment of Fulton's condition.

Fulton's worst burns covered approximately forty-five percent of his body (a number that had changed a few times already). His most severe burns were to his face, shoulder blade and waist. Over the course of the next few days, they would be doing several surgeries to tend to his burns, but for that night, they simply wanted him safe and comfortable. IVs were already started on him, and they would be flooding his body with fluids over the next twenty-four to forty-eight hours to prevent organ failure.

While he miraculously sustained little damage to his airways, they had him on a ventilator to prevent his airways from closing off. Swelling of the airway, even without the extra fluids, was one of his biggest risks at the moment and they were taking every precaution they could to help him survive the night. Tomorrow, the doctor explained, they will begin to help him heal.

I entered his room, feeling much more secure about our surroundings. He was lightly wrapped in clean bandages and a lot of the soot was gone. He still smelled faintly of gasoline, but at least I knew he was safe. His nurse was calm and reassuring, explaining that Fulton was her only patient and it was hospital policy that she not leave his room. If she had to leave, for whatever reason, another nurse would stand guard until she returned. This twenty-four-hour monitoring would continue for Fulton for several days. Eventually he graduated to sharing a nurse with one other patient, with the nurse staying either in his room or at a small station right outside his door. Later, his nurses would go from room to room between various patients as he got better. But for now, this one woman would be his guardian to keep watch over him throughout the entire night. It was nearly impossible to tear myself away from his bedside. *St. Rita, patron of impossible cases, pray for us.*

That first night was awful. The apartment was very clean—freshly painted and with new furnishings, but every sound echoed and I was uncomfortable. I felt as though I were miles from my son, though in reality he was only a few blocks away. They promised they would call if Fulton's condition turned for the worse and could pick me up if I felt a need to be there. This comforted me somewhat, but it was still a very restless night.

I called Jay and filled him in on all I knew. After more tears and prayers we exchanged a heartbreaking goodbye. The darkness pressed in around me and I quickly headed to the bathroom to ready myself for sleep. Squinting under the harsh lights, I emptied the contents of my bag onto the counter. No toothbrush or toothpaste, no hairbrush, and no deodorant. No pajamas, nothing for showering and no change of clothes in the morning. Just $20 and the granola bar I decided to save for breakfast. I swished my mouth out with the unfamiliar tasting water and I got ready for bed as best I could. *I will worry about my teeth and clothes tomorrow*, I sighed, and shivering under the sterile smelling sheet and blanket, I offered up my minor discomforts for Fulton's soul until sleep mercifully came.

***

Dear Lord, I do not know yet where You want to take us. But I trust You have our best interests in mind. Hold me close. Send me help. Strengthen me however You see fit, that I continue to love You with humility and rely on You for all things. I accept both this suffering and the charity You send with equal pleasure, for I know it all ultimately comes from Your heart. Glory be to the Father, and to the Son, and to the Holy Ghost. As it was in the beginning, is now, and ever shall be, world without end. Amen.

CHAPTER 9

"Oh! How happy is the heart that loves and
cherishes the divine will in all events!"
—*St. Francis de Sales*

I was exhausted when I entered the hospital the next morning.
Still groggy from a restless night, accompanied by an adrenaline
hangover, I was not prepared for my first day at my new job: that
of a hospital mother. Prayers were continually running through
my head as I rode the elevator to the second floor, and I
wondered what had happened while we were apart. *Will Fulton*
survive? Is he scared, or even aware of what is happening to him? Did he
realize I was not with him last night?

When I entered that hospital room the next morning, my
world was completely changed. I was no longer the mother of six,
living in Oklahoma. Now I was the mother of one suffering,
possibly dying, little boy.

I had been given basic instructions the night before about
how I was to help keep infections from spreading around the
hospital, and this morning I was instructed once again. "Infection
is one of the greatest risks to our patients," one of the nurses
explained. "We have a routine we ask all parents to abide by to
make sure germs are not spread."

The process was simple enough. Every room had an
automatic hand sanitizer close to the door. Once my hands were
sanitized, I was to pull a medical gown from a large yellow bucket

and put it on. These gowns were open in the back and already tied at the neck, reducing the amount of awkward struggling and adjusting that would have to be done as I put it on. Next came the gloves. Once properly dressed, I could enter the room. If I had to leave the room for any reason, there was a red bucket just inside the room into which I would toss the gown I wore. I put the gloves into the trash can next to the used gowns and then sanitized my hands after I left the room.

"Please tell friends and family not to send balloons, plants, cut flowers, or stuffed animals, as they could cause a spread of bacteria. Anything handed to Fulton should be disinfected, and anything he handles should be disinfected as well," the nurse paused and we looked at his unconscious, unmoving and heavily bandaged body. "But I suppose we will worry about that when the time comes."

Every nurse and doctor who entered and exited Fulton's room carefully followed the same sanitizing procedures I had to perform, as they were at even greater risk of spreading bacteria from patient to patient. Because of their careful procedures, infection was rare, and I reminded myself to refrain from bringing in anything that would not be absolutely needed each day.

The temperature turned tropical as I entered, and I felt as though I had stepped into a dimly lit sanctuary. Hushed tones, unusual smells, and the repetitive beeps and sounds of mechanical breathing calmed me somehow. *Healing will happen here*, I thought. *Lord, prepare me.*

Avoiding looking at his face, I went immediately to his left foot and caressed it as I knelt beside him. The warmth of his skin was comforting, but none of the softness that was so familiar to me could be felt through the gloves. *He is still with me, praise God!* I closed my eyes and held onto his foot as if this connection were the only thing keeping the two of us alive.

His nurse softly reviewed the night. "Fulton had a quiet night," she explained. "There were some minor issues which we took care of, and he is very sedated now, and resting. Today will be his first of many surgeries as the surgeons get a better idea of his injuries."

Slowly, I raised myself up and forced myself to gaze upon what was left of my son. He lay motionless on the bed, even more swollen than before. The vent tube was in his mouth to help him breathe and keep his airways open as the swelling continued. "Why is he so swollen?" I asked, choking back the tears.

"We have found that flooding the system with fluids within the first twenty-four hours of a burn actually helps prevent organ failure. He is also on some medication to help prevent that, but the fluids are vital." *Lord help me.* I hadn't even thought that organ failure would have been a concern! I suddenly realized how completely ignorant I was on burns. "He is a little alarming to see now, but the swelling will go down in a few days," she said reassuringly. Indeed, he was difficult to look at. He still had the loose bandages and patches of soot on his good skin, and I still detected the faint odor of singed hair when I leaned close to him. My stomach churned as I recalled the stench of gasoline and scorched flesh the day before. "How did you sleep?" she asked.

"Not well," I admitted. "I was not comfortable being so far from the hospital. I just feel like I need to be closer to him right now." I felt like I was asking for a miracle and being utterly selfish, but my heart had slowly died every moment I was away from him the night before.

She nodded. "I will see what I can do for you. I can't make any promises, but there may be some options available." I thanked her and she said her goodbyes to both me and to Fulton, as it was time for the night nurses' shift to end. She went to the front desk and discussed Fulton's case with the day nurse, waved one last time to me, and left us in the capable hands of Fulton's new nurse.

Soon, I was called out to the main desk to discuss the plans for the day. After disrobing and disposing of my protective gear, I tried my best to put on my business face and concentrate, but it was difficult to sift through the emotion, urgency, and strange vocabulary. "Fulton has been moved up to the front of the line this morning for the first round of debridement and to insert a few tubes," the head nurse explained. "His surgeon is already waiting. Please initial here, giving permission to do the procedures we intend to do for the day, and here, where you give us permission to give him blood, should he need it, and right here, acknowledging that he may die on the operating table."

Blinking back the tears, my pen faltered. *If I do not initial this, will my denial mean he will survive?* The head nurse cleared his throat. "We cannot proceed without your signatures. This form simply lays out what we are going to do and lists the risks inherent with each procedure. You will be doing this for every single surgery over the next few months while you are here."

Months. There was that word again. I initialed the last line and began to focus on what he had just said. I knew we would be there awhile, but up to this point I had reserved a level of denial for myself. But now I had to translate 'awhile' to actual calendar days.

"So, what exactly happened?" he asked as he clipped what was to be the first of dozens of surgical consent forms into a black three-ring binder.

My mind was still reeling with what I had already seen and been told this morning. "There was a gas can, and I guess it was too close to the burning barrel or something. It exploded . . ." I faltered, realizing it sounded rather lame, but did not care. "I was in the house when it happened."

He jotted down some notes. "Alright. Thank you." And then, in a gentle, less businesslike tone he reassured, "We are going to take good care of your son."

Paperwork completed, I disinfected myself and reentered Fulton's room as the anesthesiologist and nurses prepped him to be rolled into surgery. I gave his perfect little foot a squeeze and gently kissed his toes. "I love you, Fulton," I whispered. His tiny body looked so delicate and vulnerable, surrounded by the adult-sized hospital bed, breathing machine and IV. They wheeled him out, leaving me alone in the now stark and silent room.

I sat on the large, wooden rocking chair in his room and waited for his return. I hadn't bothered showering that morning. I had no toiletries and was still wearing the clothes I arrived in the night before. *Good grief. I'm a mess!*

My clunky homesteading Ariat boots were splattered with mud. I had on one of my poor fitting brown denim skirts, complete with paint stains, and Jay's oversized gray sweatshirt. I was dressed for homestead work—not the hospital, and while I didn't particularly care what people thought of my grungy outfit, I felt unclean.

"Why don't you use this time to take care of the extra stuff you need to get in order while you are waiting for Fulton to return," the new nurse suggested. "I suggest you get started with Housing and Transportation, as they will be able to help you with most of your physical needs. You will be meeting with your Care Coordinator this morning and she will help you make sense of what will be happening here."

Every patient is assigned a care coordinator who helps explain and keep track of the care given to the patient. She explained to me the roles of the people at the security desk. I was to sign in and out each day, noting where I planned to be. They in turn would give me a sticker noting that I was a visitor for the day. If at any point, day or night, I needed to go somewhere, the security personnel would take me there in one of the hospital's vans.

Housing and Transportation was also an important part of the whole Shriner's genius. The women in that department kept in contact with Fulton's supporting Shriner lodge, coordinating what housing they would be able to offer me. I was relieved to hear that I not only was given a place to stay, but meal cards as well.

And much to my relief, they also gave me clothing. There was a fully stocked closet with hundreds of articles of clothing for all sizes. "Take two or three outfits for you to cycle through," the woman explained. "They are yours to keep or donate them back to us as you wish. Here is a bag with all the toiletries you will probably need. We also have laundry detergent and a free laundry room down the hall for you to use to wash your clothes." I was overwhelmed. *Thank you, Lord!*

I chose two outfits, hoping to be able to purchase a few of my own items fairly soon. As if reading my mind, she added, "Every Saturday morning we take a few parents to Walmart to pick up whatever they need. Just come in and sign up and we will arrange the rest."

Clothes, toiletries, and meal cards in hand, I then spoke to the psychologist who was assigned to Fulton.

"Fulton will thankfully remember nothing of the first week or more of his stay here," the doctor explained. "But he will have many memories and experiences that will cause him trauma. I work closely with the rest of the team to make sure Fulton has the best possible emotional outcome, and we can quickly address any issues you are having as well."

Emotional trauma? I was still trying to wrap my head around the fact I was going to be there for several months. Somehow the thought of physical trauma was not as upsetting as knowing somewhere down the road Fulton would be suffering emotionally. Soothing a hurt child was easy. But fixing emotional wounds seemed far more difficult.

After speaking with the psychologist, I returned to the room to wait for Fulton. The room itself looked extremely large now that his bed was gone. One wall, where the head of his bed would be, was covered with medical equipment, plugs, lights and knobs. Adjacent to that was a wall with a window looking out towards the UTMB hospital across the street. Our floor was even with the height of the tops of the palm trees lining the street, and I frequently watched the palm leaves sway in the cool winter breeze. This wall was also lined with a long counter with cabinets above and drawers below, containing every medical supply we could ever need. The nurse remained seated at this counter, constantly reviewing or entering information about Fulton's status on the computer. This was also where she would prepare Fulton's bandages while we chatted each day.

As the days wore on, I would help her by massaging the petroleum-based antibiotic ointments into strips of gauze. Any activities I could do to feel useful was a balm to my soul, but that first day, I just watched and waited.

There was a full bathroom on the next wall, complete with a bathtub, and a glass partition into the next room, which was blacked out for privacy. The main wall running parallel to the hallway was completely glass, giving me a chance to passively watch how the medical staff operated.

There were about eighteen rooms on the ICU floor, wrapping around three sides of the nurses' station in the center. Every room had a glass wall just as ours did, but the size of the rooms varied. Fulton was in one of the larger rooms, and I observed that the newer and more severe cases were given the most space. Some patients actually occupied two rooms, when their needs demanded. Most were in beds or cribs, and a few had to be strapped into beds that flipped up and around while the child was safely strapped in. I was immediately thankful Fulton was on a regular hospital bed and vowed to try not to lament our own suffering.

A tall, kind-looking woman entered the room with some files. "Mrs. Poppe?"

I nodded.

She introduced herself and explained her role at the hospital. "I am part of the research department here at Shriners. I am so sorry about your son's accident. It must be quite a shock to be here."

We chatted a few minutes, getting to know each other and then she asked, "You are aware that Shriner's is a research hospital, right? Your son will be receiving the most up-to-date, expert care available to pediatric burn patients. We are known around the world for our groundbreaking studies and procedures, and doctors around the world come here to learn from our head surgeon and the head of our research department."

I was liking what I was hearing so far.

"I know it feels too early to be making these types of decisions, but we would like to ask you to consider allowing Fulton to be a part of our research. It is rare when we get a Caucasian patient in here with the types of burns he has, and other patients could really benefit from whatever we can learn through your son's healing process."

Her own son had been a patient at Shriners many years earlier. He suffered burns on 99% of his body, with only a tiny patch of skin on one foot and one armpit unharmed. As these two sites were the only two from which they could harvest skin, he remained in Shriner's ICU for over a year and not only survived, but thrived. "He benefited from the research our hospital had done years before his accident, and I know that had my son been burned today, his recovery time would have been even shorter because of all we have learned since his release.

"Not too long ago, it was understood that for every percentage of a child's body that was burned, he would spend at least that many days in the ICU. But we have been able to cut that number in half!" she said, proudly.

Amazing! I still had no idea what it would take to heal Fulton, but I could tell by seeing the other patients that his recovery would be difficult.

She then explained to me the research they wanted to do with Fulton, but it was too much to take in. She apologized many times for asking me so soon, but one of the studies required Fulton to begin within just a few short days after his accident. At best, all I could tell her was that I would talk to Jay about it and get back with her. I felt sorry for her, knowing how uncomfortable she was coming to me so soon, yet feeling the pressure to begin the research as soon as possible.

I just wasn't ready. We did eventually consent to two of their research programs and are happy we were able to make a small but helpful contribution to their studies.

Fulton's surgery was finally complete and they wheeled him back into the room. He was still on the vent and many medications were now connected to his picc line, each one separately connected to their own monitors, electronically tracking what the medication was and the rate of dosage Fulton was to receive.

A completely unrecognizable child lay in the bed before me. I was overwhelmed at what I saw and did not know where to start. At least his nose was now identifiable by the three tubes threaded into one of his nostrils. "What are these tubes for?" I asked.

"Two of the tubes go to his stomach. One for nutrition and the other for medications that can't go through his picc line," the nurse explained. "The third one goes to his airway, which we use to suction out the fluid that builds up in his lungs."

I felt like I should be asking more questions, but I just sat down in the rocking chair and stared, letting the medical staff tell me what I needed to know. A tall, dark haired man entered the room and introduced himself as Fulton's main surgeon. He was following his case closely, and all medical decisions would go through him from now on, until Fulton was sent home.

I did not know it then, but he is exactly the kind of doctor to whom you would want your loved ones entrusted. Two years after Fulton's accident, a mother to another one of his patients posted a moving picture of him at the deathbed of her son, and sang his praises:

> *'06/28/15 10:30 p.m. See this man? Let me tell you about him. He did such a great job helping Adam. We were blessed to have him as his doctor. When Adam coded the first time on that day, the doctor was in his room, checking on him, as he normally did several times a day. Every day. Adam coded three more times that night, and he never left his side. Even after Adam passed away, he couldn't bring himself to leave. This picture shows him preparing Adam to be removed from his room. He didn't have to do that—he could have simply told us goodbye and gone home, leaving this job to the nursing staff. But, he waited for us to take our time and tell Adam goodbye. This man is the most caring doctor I have ever known. We will love him, always."*

I thank God for placing Fulton under the watchful eye of this good doctor and pray for him by name.

After our quick introductions, the doctor asked, "Was there an accelerant involved when the accident happened? And how quickly was the fire put out?"

"Yes, our gas can exploded. I don't know how long it took, though. I heard the explosion, glanced out the window and did not see him at that time. Then my daughter told me Fulton was on fire, so I looked again and that was when I saw him. By the time I ran to the door, my husband was already on top of him and the flames were out."

He nodded gravely. "Gasoline fires can range from 1000 to 1200 degrees and cause severe damage in an instant, which would explain the severity of his burns that occurred in such a short time. Here is what we know so far . . ."

He then gave me his assessment of Fulton's condition: In summation, Fulton received third degree burns to over 90% of his face and about 50% of his head, patches on his arms and left leg, and his entire left shoulder blade, patches on his chest and his entire lower abdomen and waistband and all around his waistband area with the worst of that area being in the front. These sites officially totaled 43% of his body. The rest of his body was covered in first and second degree burns, except for his left leg which was fairly burn free.

All his wounds on his body were covered in thick layers of the medicated gauze like the ones the nurse was preparing earlier. These were literally stapled to his body to keep them in place. Larger wads of this gauze, called bolsters, sometimes measuring the size of softballs or larger, had been sewn onto the surrounding salvageable skin behind his neck and shoulders covering those wounds as well, causing him to lie in an unnatural position on his bed.

Beneath all these bandages were the wounds they tended to that morning. They performed what is called a debridement procedure, cleaning the wounds by using tiny razors to remove the dead flesh one layer at a time. When they got to a layer that began to bleed, they stopped and moved on to another spot. It is a painstaking procedure, taking hours to complete, and would have to be repeated every few days.

Debridement is important, as they had to make sure they removed every portion of dead flesh that remained. Sometimes flesh that was living during one procedure died off before the next, so all areas would have to be closely monitored. They put Fulton on a surgical schedule of every three or four days, depending on how he was tolerating these procedures.

Depending on the wound, they would either cover the area with pig skin or cadaver skin, or leave it as it was. All wounds except his face were then covered with the moist, medicated bandages. The pig and cadaver skin was used to simply cover the wounds until the living flesh was ready to take on its own skin grafts. These coverings helped keep infections at bay and told the doctors how the flesh beneath the patches were doing. If the patches did not stay on, it was an indicator that there was additional dead flesh underneath. I made sure that every time Fulton returned to the room with cadaver skin, I offered up a prayer of thanks to the donor and a prayer for his or her soul.

The doctor concluded his assessment. "The areas around his eyes are fairly burn free. He seemed to have protected them during the fire, which was very wise."

My stomach rose as I recalled the scene once again. My little boy engulfed in flames, moving in slow motion, his hands moving to his eyes to cover them. *Fulton's Guardian Angel, I thank you for inspiring him to protect himself as he was able.* "His lips are not too bad either. He must have sucked them in, or maybe his wrists helped protect them. The fewer injuries around the mouth, the better." He then gestured towards Fulton's right hand, now thickly bandaged. "We will watch his fingers daily for signs of tissue and bone dying off. If that happens, I wanted to prepare you for the possibility of having to amputate some of his fingers. We will watch his nose as well, and we are hopeful we will not have to remove portions of that."

It was too much to take in by myself and my heart cried out to my husband, six hundred miles away. *I wish you could be here to help me sort through this.* I craved his strong arms around me, to protect me from the terrifying story this surgeon was telling.

But he continued. "I am afraid we cannot do much for his ears at this point. There are parts that will probably be salvaged, but we won't know how much for several days. We have to let the tissue do what it needs to do and see what we are left with."

My heart was in agony. *He did not understand. Didn't the doctor know how cute his big elf ears were? And that tiny nose? The way he squinted his eyes when he smiled? Did he not realize that with every debridement procedure, he would be forever taking away a cherished part of my little boy?*

Aside from some additional scrubbing on the two tiny unburned portions of Fulton's face, they left his face alone. And unlike the rest of his body, there were very few bandages on his face. "Why is his face so exposed?" I managed to ask, as I eyed the glistening bruised colored skin coverings they placed where his face should be.

"The severity of his wounds are such that we decided it was best to take a wait and see approach," the surgeon explained. "We can see more quickly what is happening if it remains uncovered. And later, when we begin grafting his skin, the fewer facial grafts we have to do, the better, and it is difficult to tell so early on how much tissue will actually survive. We will begin working on his face over the next several days and weeks— whenever we decide it should be done." This explanation made little sense to me at the time, but I would later understand what he meant.

Fully aware I was in no state of mind to ask any intelligent questions, I allowed the doctor to wrap up his overall assessment of Fulton and move on. He gave the nurse a few instructions and left, leaving me thoroughly beaten and broken. I collapsed into the rocking chair and took a long look at my son.

Fulton's sweet angelic face was swollen beyond recognition and I could not believe the monstrosity of damage and pain my son was enduring. Aside from the patches by his eyes, there was no skin left. Just varying layers of the dermis and hypodermis underneath, all covered with temporary skin. He had no obvious facial features to help me recognize him as my son. The vent marked where his mouth was, and the three medication and feeding tubes entered his nose. The swelling by this point was so marked, there was only a faint difference between his face and neck, and absolutely no natural peaks and valleys of a normal face. No cheekbones, no eyelids, no bridge of his nose. No Fulton.

I began a slow grieving process, as each day revealed to me how little of his face they were going to be able to save. He did have eyelids and his lips, and so far they did not think they would have to amputate his little nose, and these were the hopeful signs to which I clung. With most of his ears dying off, how different was he going to look? It was difficult to imagine. It felt superficial to even consider his appearance at that point, but my mother's heart just longed to caress his sweet baby cheeks just one more time. The very thought took my breath away.

Partial Care Pages Entry: January 12

We are in desperate need of prayers—I will not lie. I have been entrusted with a task far beyond my capabilities and we will be here for several months, far away from home. All my trust has been placed in the hands of Our Lord and Our Lady, as only they will get me through this.

Please, please pray for Fulton! And pray for my dear sweet husband Jay who wants nothing more than to be here with us, but can't due to his own injuries.

Computer time is very limited here, but I will try to post daily if I can.

I will attempt to get through the hundreds of messages, posts and emails that have been sent to me—forgive me if I do not respond to them all! But please know that every word of every prayer is cherished.

God is good! Always! God bless!

***

Sweet Jesus, suffering the scourging, I offer You the pain my son suffers, along with his disfigurement, as a love offering of acceptance to Your holy will. Sweet Mary, Our Sorrowful Mother, be my guide as the sword of my own son's passion pierces my heart. Amen.

CHAPTER 10

"The Creator of our bodies knew what He was doing."
—St. Cyril of Jerusalem

The weight of our cross increased as the days slowly passed. About four days after the accident, they announced they were going to attempt to remove Fulton from the vent. This was a good thing, they told me, as they would be able to do much more for him once he was free and breathing on his own. I was asked to leave the room, which I gladly did, and headed up to the cafeteria for some breakfast and made some phone calls.

The cafeteria was on the seventh floor, and while the weather was beginning to clear up a little, it was still gray and foggy. I could see a little past the iron railings outside and even the outline of some houses and trees far below. But the ocean was still beyond my view. "Please pray for Fulton," I told my mother. "They are removing him from the vent as we speak."

We chatted a few more minutes and I headed back down to his room. Before I even made it inside the doors of the ICU, I was abruptly stopped by a waiting nurse. "I'm sorry, Mrs. Poppe, but you can't go into his room yet. He didn't do so well on his own so we are reinserting the ventilator."

The nurse looked concerned, and as soon as I understood I could not see Fulton yet, she rushed back to his room for an update. Hopes crushed, I lowered myself onto a chair and stared at the floor.

A man's voice broke the silence. "That was your boy?"

I shrugged, still unclear as to what exactly happened. "I guess."

A thin, poorly dressed man smiled at me. His dark, weathered face was friendly, and he moved comfortably about as if he were welcoming me into his home. He shook my hand and introduced himself, then said, "We were having my daughter's vent removed today right after they were going to work on your boy. I guess he stopped breathing and just about everyone rushed out of our room to take care of him. All those nurses just poured out from everywhere! Scared all of us parents!"

I closed my eyes, attempting to shake the image from my mind. *How terrified he must have been. Unable to think clearly from his sedation, not understanding what has happened to him or where he was. Did he cry out for me inside, and I was nowhere near him? Or was his struggle to take a life-giving breath the only thing that consumed him?* A mother's heart can only take so much. I pushed all these thoughts away and focused on a prayer of thanksgiving instead.

Eventually they called me back. What used to be a quiet, dimly lit room was now uncomfortably bright and still bustling with doctors and nurses as they continued to monitor him and update his charts. Although he frequently broke through levels of sedation that would bring down a full grown man, Fulton was at least temporarily deeply sedated and unresponsive. His oxygen percentage remained in the 80s and he showed no signs of the drama that occurred an hour before. I kissed his good foot and sat quietly by his bedside, drained. *I almost lost you again, little guy. Hold on!*

Slowly, the medical staff began to trickle out until, at last, it was just the nurse, Fulton and myself. She dimmed the lights and quietly receded into the background, allowing Fulton and me to reconnect. By this time I had grown more accustomed to his features, and I gazed at his face.

His ears were very curled and there did not seem to be much they could salvage at that point. "We have an artist who does miraculous work creating all sorts of prosthetics for us," a nurse had mentioned earlier that day. "One day, as he gets bigger, we can fit him with ears that will look almost natural!"

I knew this was supposed to make me feel better, and it did on a certain level, but it was still alarming to hear such things explained to me in such a matter-of-fact way. Did the nurse not know how strange that sounded? To think that we will be tied to this hospital for his entire childhood, a future filled with reconstructive surgeries and prosthetics, therapies and medications. It was overwhelming.

But amid the horror were signs of hope. The swelling was beginning to go down a little, and I could almost make out the bridge of his nose. His lips were taking on a more normal shape and were not rubbing so much on the tubes in his nose. I could even see a bit of his eyelids now, singed eyelashes and all.

Blinking away the tears, I recalled the night before, standing over him, speaking softly and trying to get him to respond to my words. There was a little facial twitch! I spoke to him again, encouraging him to open his eyes and look at me. Slowly, his left eye opened, but with great difficulty. His eyelids were still engorged, but there, beneath the horror of his little face was a perfect blue eye. "There he is!" I softly cooed. "Hello Fulton! Mama's here. I love you!" He was with me only for a moment, but that beauty beneath all the suffering gave me new hope. And I cried.

I stood by his side once again, this time no hope of seeing his beautiful blue eye, but he was still alive and I was thankful.

Even with the vent in place, his oxygen numbers frequently fell to the mid 60%, and after turning up his vent to 50%, the respiratory specialist hovered just outside his room for the rest of the day.

Already on high alert, the eerie sound of air being forced out of his lungs as he coughed on the ventilator immediately put me on edge. Soon Fulton's temperature rose above 103 degrees and the nurse began drawing blood when she removed fluid from his lungs. While terrifying for me, the doctors took all of this in stride.

The nurse explained what was happening. "When an airway is damaged through inhaling fumes and scorching air, the dead cells in the airway will begin to slough off and enter the lungs, putting the patient at risk for pneumonia. Fulton was still unable to sit up and move around, which increases his chances of fluids building up in his lungs. I am not really surprised pneumonia is settling in."

Her matter-of-fact bedside manner helped me stay focused on the task at hand. I had decided at this point to stop watching the readings on the monitors and gave it all up to Our Lord. *You brought us safely to this point; You will see us through.*

Care Pages Entry Posted Jan 12, 2013

I have an easier time looking at his face—I am resigned to God's will and steeling myself for the torturous months ahead. (These early days, I am told, are the easiest to get through. Lord have mercy!) My personal plan of attack is to place myself next to Our Blessed Mother as she knelt at the foot of the Cross. There is not much I can do for Fulton in the way of comfort right now, but I hold his good foot and kiss it often, joining my sorrows with Mary as she watched at the foot of the Cross.

I will be contacting the Fulton Sheen Foundation and will be placing Fulton officially under the patronage and care of Venerable Fulton Sheen, that his powerful prayers may be the catalyst for whatever miracles Our Lord has planned. All glory to God!

I know that it will be a rocky road ahead, but I also know God is very much with us. God's love sometimes looks ugly on the surface, but many imperfections are being refined here, and we will come out far better souls than what we were when we first arrived.

I am so overwhelmed at the support and love pouring out for my little guy. The tears flow freely here, but so do the hugs, and I am ever so grateful to everyone. I am continually amazed at the amount of love and goodness there is in this world.

The nurses here are so wonderful, and I am getting to know the respiratory physician so well I can joke with him. (Anything to lighten the mood!) Scary stuff going on here, but everyone's prayers are covering us and are as thick as the fog outside. I feel Our Lady's mantle covering us both. But it is still painfully lonely. None of the other mothers here speak English, so I spend a lot of time in silence, just loving Our Lord and little Fulton.

They removed several staples in his hands and will probably remove all the gauze and mesh coverings they had to staple onto his torso and arms tomorrow morning. The doctor wants to assess what all they will be attending to for his next surgery on Monday. I am anxious to hear their assessment of his poor little face. As each day passes, I can definitely tell what will have to go (the skin is completely dead at this point) but am still unclear on what gets to stay.

They took me to Walmart today, where I picked up some precious basics and am now resting more comfortably overall. I am getting used to the ups and downs and am learning that staying on an even keel is best. If I based my emotions on the readings on the monitors, I'd go crazy.

Thank you, thank you, thank you once again for all the prayers you all are drumming up for us! I will post again soon—if these computers let me!

I love you all! God is so good!

Indeed God is always good, and I clung to this truth. *Lord, I trust in Your plan completely. But if it be Your will, please heal Fulton.* Day after day, he lay on that hospital bed and I had no way of knowing how aware he was of his surroundings. "Can he hear me when I talk to him?"

"Probably, depending on how sedated he is," the nurse answered. "We have him maxed out right now and he still breaks through. It never hurts to talk to him, though." She smiled, and I could tell she had had this conversation many times before with other parents who were anxious to bond with their children.

As if on cue, Fulton began to move his foot. Then the rest of his body grew restless and we leaped to the side of his bed to restrain him if needed. Any movement put strain on his bolsters which could either tear the staples out, loosen the cadaver skin from his wounds, or move his vent tube, causing damage to his airway.

He arched his back, suddenly, and like a fish out of water, began violently writhing in his bed. "Fulton!" the nurse said firmly, "you can't move around like that. You are going to hurt yourself!" We tried our best to hold him still but he desperately thrashed around. "He is a fighter!" his nurse said in amazement. "I have never seen such a small child come out of this level of sedation so often!"

Fulton's lips began to move, but no sound would come, his voice hindered by the ventilator tube. *Dear Lord, he is becoming more aware of his surroundings.* He must have been scared. And in so much pain. What could I say to him, since I did not know what he was trying to say to me?

And then, he began to cry. His little face contorted as a child's face does when crying—forehead and eyebrow muscles coming together, jaw opening in a silent wail, his raw tissue amplifying the raw emotions he was feeling beneath it all. There were no tears. No sounds. But we had no doubt what he was feeling at that moment. Beneath the bandages, the patches of cadaver skin, oozing blisters, and blood-red glistening skinless tissue was a tiny little boy in agony, his very soul crying out to for his mother who was not allowed to hold him in her arms. And at that point, I surrendered to tears myself.

The nurse, satisfied he was done moving around, adjusted some of his medications and quietly returned to her computer, allowing me to comfort him as best I could. *My Sorrowful Mother, be with me here.*

I simply spoke to him in soft tones, telling him I was with him and that he would be feeling better soon. "You had an accident," I explained to him. I had no way of knowing how much he remembered from one waking moment to the next, so I always started with the basics. "You will start to feel better soon. You are in a safe place, surrounded by people who are taking good care of you. I am staying with you, too, OK?" My words seemed so useless. What could I possibly say to a four-year-old who is suffering so much? His cries seemed to slow and his breathing surrendered to the ventilator once again.

The nurse nodded and smiled. "Good job, Mom," she whispered.

I could barely see him through my tears. "Try to rest if you can, to make your body stronger." I reassured him again that he was in a safe place and then told him, "I can see that God is fixing you, Fulton. We will try to be patient and let God do His work."

From a very young age, I trained my children to trust in Our Lord in a very safe way. This early training proved to be another blessing to us as Fulton healed, as our faith was tried and tested on many occasions. Whenever my children had a tummy ache or a scrape on their knee, I would tell them "God will fix it!" and He always proved me right. This early training has resulted in many moments of joy when my children would peel back a Band-aid and squeal "Look Mama! God is fixing me!" as they watch their cuts and scrapes slowly heal. Or when they wake up in the morning, fever broken, exclaiming "God fixed me when I was asleep!" We would always pray a prayer of thanksgiving for God's healing powers, and I would add my own silent prayer of thanks to Him for showing me how to strengthen their faith in Him in such simple ways.

Knowing how our bodies were so wonderfully made by Almighty God, this was not a lie, but rather a different way of looking at the body's natural ability to heal itself. Who created our immune system? Our skin? And the entire healing process? God. And whenever my children were injured, I reminded them that God's healing power was hard at work, making them better.

So, when I spoke to Fulton in the hospital, I reminded him that the doctors and nurses were listening to God's wisdom and participating with God to make him better. "Every day, God is fixing you more and more! His angels are hard at work, too. We just have to be patient. You will feel so much better in a few days."

I found different ways of keeping his mind occupied when he was conscious. When he was anxious I would sing him the Hail Mary prayer to a tune I had made up years before, which used to lull him to sleep before the accident. I played a recording of Fur Elise my son Ryan always played on the piano at home, hoping the familiar tune would keep him distracted from his pain and give him a sense of comfort. I would describe the palm trees outside his window, and tell him the leaves were waving to him in the wind, cheering him on, and tried to build a sense of excitement about the first time he would be able to see the tops of the trees himself. And when his pain became unbearable, I wept as I prayed while massaging his one good foot, saddened that it was the only physical comfort I could offer. Thankfully, with the help of the medications, he recovered quicker than I, and I was told he will have no memory of this stage at all. Thanks be to God! But those days will remain in my heart forever.

There were days when we truly thought he would give up. How much suffering can one child endure? Especially a child who could not possibly know how to suffer well?

Care Pages Entry Posted Jan 15, 2013

Cassandra just called. Urgent prayers are needed. Fulton is having trouble keeping his oxygen levels up. He has crashed twice today already with levels in the low 50s. Respiratory specialists came running immediately and brought him back up again, but they haven't figured out yet why it's doing this. Unfortunately, they can't focus on the burns until they get the respiratory problem under control. So, for the next two days or so, we need to focus on this. Please pray for better oxygen levels.

Fulton also developed a bleeding skin rash on all of his good skin, causing a further delay in his surgeries.

Care Pages Entry Posted Jan 16, 2013

Fulton's skin was biopsied today, so hopefully we will have an answer on the mysterious rash by Friday morning. Meanwhile they stopped two of the three antibiotics they were giving him, and replaced them with one new one. Poor little body will never be the same after all these antibiotics! But I am trying not to worry about that now. The respiratory specialists are narrowing his breathing issues down a little. He is having great difficulty exhaling, which apparently makes his CO2 levels too high. They suspect a few different reasons for this, but are hesitant to make a final diagnosis until further testing is done. Despite all the sedatives they are giving him, he still comes out of sedation from time to time and thrashes like a wild man (Typical Fulton behavior!). Unfortunately, with all the tubes, IVs, etc., and with his injuries, this is not safe at all, though, so we continue to watch him like a hawk and pounce the minute his toes start to wiggle. His good foot is now completely wrapped and they fitted him with a 'boot' to prevent his tendons from shrinking any more than they already have. He must get off the ventilator soon, or a whole new pile of problems will start to occur.

The doctors and nurses spent a lot of time educating me on all aspects of burn care to better prepare me for what we may be faced with as time went on. "No other injuries cause the sort of suffering and devastation a burn does," one of his night nurses explained. "Organs shut down, childhood osteoporosis sets in, testosterone stops being produced and growth stops, the body cannibalizes itself to fuel the healing process, eyesight can be impaired, diabetes can begin as the child grows, kidney and liver damage can occur from trying to process the toxins released into the body, severe heart damage can occur due to the elevated blood pressure and heart rate caused by the hypermetabolic state to which the body switches." The list was alarming.

"What are Fulton's chances of surviving?" I hesitantly asked.

The nurse glanced at Fulton as she answered. "It is hard to tell. Sometimes we have lost patients with a little over 10% of burns on their bodies. And we have seen patients with burns over

90% of their bodies walk out of here. There is no way of knowing. No guarantees. But I will tell you that Fulton is under the best care possible." Her words reassured me.

"And what about new skin growth? Will that happen on its own?"

Her answer was complicated. "The skin grafts will not grow like regular skin and he will need to have more surgeries as he grows. Children literally grow out of their grafted skin. But we have learned that as long as either sweat or oil glands or even hair follicles have survived, the skin is able to be regenerated on its own surrounding the immediate area around them. So if there is a patch of glands and follicles that have survived, his skin can grow back in those areas. But most times, in burns this bad, there are not enough surviving glands to make much of a difference."

"Can I donate my skin to him?" I asked, hoping we would be a match.

"Unfortunately no. Skin is not like other organs and the body will reject any other skin but its own. We used to take skin cells from patients and sent it off to be grown, but we have found that this skin has a high chance of turning cancerous so we try not to go that route unless we have to. So, our best bet is to keep harvesting from healthy areas on his body."

So be it. Knowing Fulton was benefitting from decades of intense and meticulous research, I once again resigned myself to simply watch and wait. And hope.

I stopped keeping track of the number of surgeries Fulton had endured, once the number reached thirty. And the number continues to rise. Countless times he returns to me from the operating room with wounds that look as though they could never heal. And yet, by God's great wisdom in His creation, those wounds heal every time. I am continually amazed, but Fulton never is. And his ongoing, steadfast faith reminds me of a moment that occurred only a few months after the accident.

Fulton was recovering from yet another surgery and the large donor site on his thigh was visibly healing. Our friend Heather was visiting and she saw this wound. "Your leg looks so much better!" she exclaimed. "The doctors are doing such a great job fixing you."

"No," Fulton responded without missing a beat, "God is fixing me."

To this day, Fulton seems to understand that while the doctors certainly have helped him tremendously, it is through God's wondrous creation of the human body and the many gifts God has given them that his healing has actually taken place. And that ultimately God has chosen to heal him as He sees fit. In His time and at His good pleasure.

***

Oh Lord, indeed we are fearfully and wonderfully made! I thank You for reminding us on a daily basis how much You care for us through the natural healing that takes place in our bodies each day. Through Your great design, I see how our bodies were created to heal themselves, and even when one such as Fulton requires a little extra help, I am still in awe at how intricately involved You are in every action the doctors take, and how their research results in a deeper understanding of how miraculous our bodies truly are. Continue to surprise us. Continue to humble us. And continue to teach us all we are to know of the miracle of our creation. Amen.

CHAPTER 11

"A glove is not more fitted to a hand or a sword to a scabbard than what He does and ordains in us and for us is suited to our strength and capabilities, so that everything may serve to our advantage and perfection if we but cooperate with the designs of his providence."
—*Father Jean Baptiste Saint-Jure*

Shriner's operates under the assumption that most patients will heal faster if they are under the care of a parent. Therefore, all of their care is focused on this milestone. Their care philosophy was explained to me like this: In other hospitals, burn patients remain in the ICU for awhile, are moved to a regular hospital room to continue to receive their needed care, and are then sent home. At Shriners, they completely bypass the regular hospital stay and release the patient to the parent's care as soon as they have healed enough to leave the ICU. The patient remains near the hospital in a more homelike environment and must return daily to receive the many treatments and therapies they need so that they can eventually be discharged and sent home.

Parental involvement is vital to the overall wellbeing of the children and they include the parents in almost all of the medical decisions that need to be made. They provide constant opportunities for the parents to learn how to clean and wrap wounds, administer medications, and do general patient care procedures. I helped change his bed and his diapers, suctioned his mouth when he threw up, and pumped medicine and liquid vitamins into his feeding tubes. As he improved, they trained me how to properly care for his wounds and grafts in the tubroom.

Tubroom appointments caused the most suffering for Fulton, and he still to this day fears he will have to return there. Every tubroom day in the hospital began with a high level of heartbreaking drama. The nurses made sure he had his pain and anti-anxiety medications in his system well before it was his turn to be washed, though it is hard to say if they actually did him any good.

"I know it is hard," the nurses would explain, "but these are necessary steps we need to take to get him released to your care."

Honestly, I had mixed feelings about that. I had to show the tubroom nurses I was strong enough to scrub him properly, and not go easy on him. If I proved myself, they would release him to my care. Nevertheless, seeing the pain caused by the tubroom made it difficult to push through the task.

Furthermore, as much as I wanted Fulton released to stay with me, and even though I longed for the day when I could cook him food that he was used to, curl up on the couch with him to watch a movie, and begin some semblance of a regular life once again, being his sole provider for medical care away from Shriners was terrifying. Each day at the hospital was extremely tiring, and I desperately needed time at night to unwind and get some sleep. Nevertheless, only one month after his accident, they decided Fulton was ready for his next level of care, and I soon understood what the nurses meant when they said that the first few weeks in the ICU were to be the easiest.

When we were in the hospital, tubroom time was every morning. But after they released him to my care, we had additional bathing and bandage changing every evening which I struggled to complete in the Ronald McDonald House. We would have dinner, unwrap his wounds, then wash and rewrap them again. We would finally crash at about 11 p.m., only to have to wake at 4:30 a.m. the next morning to begin the scrubbing process again back at the hospital.

On a perfect day, we would arrive at the hospital tubroom by 6 a.m. with his bandages already soaked, softened, and ready to be removed. Fulton would sit on a towel inside a stainless steel tub and allow me to vigorously scrub his wound sites using soft lap rags and lots of Ivory liquid soap. There was a constant supply of running water through a hose that gently rinsed him off. I would then carefully towel him off, wrap him up to keep him warm, and wait for the team of doctors to come in and assess his progress. There were anywhere from two to six doctors at these check-ups, depending on the day and the issues we were having.

After his daily assessment, the various ointments or medications needed were applied to each wound. I would then cut pieces of nonstick gauze exactly the same shape as his wounds and apply these pieces over his wounds. This step was important, I was told, since the medicine on the gauze could actually make the wounds larger if it got onto already healed skin. After this, I would wrap his limbs in gauze to keep them clean, which were then covered with Ace bandages. For several weeks, his entire body was wrapped, except for his privates and the calf of his one good leg, so this procedure took a tremendous amount of time.

That was how the morning procedure was supposed to go on a perfect day. Because Fulton was so terrified of the tubroom, he never sat in the tub, but spent the entire time screaming and trying to climb out. For some reason, each little piece of non-stick gauze I had to place over the wounds stuck to him like superglue and therefore required extensive soaking, soaping, and scrubbing just to get them off. Then I had to go back and actually wash the wounds themselves, removing any pieces of tissue that were not healing properly, all the while causing him unbearable pain.

Even though we used the softest wash rags possible, older burn patients describe the tubroom washings as feeling like burning sandpaper on an open wound. The gentlest touch would send Fulton into fits, and he screamed as though I were slowly killing him. Similar shrieks and sobs always came from the tubroom next to us each day, and it was heartbreaking to be surrounded by such utter agony. It was even worse to have to be the one inflicting such pain.

Prayers, apologies, and bribes were used each morning to get us through the tubroom appointment. Then after the doctors saw him, we would begin the bandaging process. He was fairly cooperative for this part, although it was still quite painful for him to endure. We practiced brave breaths and took our time, as I used this time to start "making up" with him for the earlier struggles. He was mad. I was exhausted. And it was only 8:45 a.m.

After the tubroom, we headed up to the cafeteria where I would have to once again resort to prayers and bribes to get him to eat. His body was in a hypermetabolic state which meant that his body was basically cannibalizing itself to get what it needed to heal his burns. His heart rate and blood pressure were dangerously high because of this and I had to do everything I could to make sure he ate over twice the normal calories required for a four-year-old boy, just to maintain his weight.

Unfortunately, maintenance was not enough. This trial release to my care was to make sure he could actually gain weight in a non-medical environment. Shriners will not send a child home until they are comfortable knowing the patient's hypermetabolic condition was well managed. So in addition to charting all of his daily medications, I had to chart every bite of food that went into his body, as well as anything he might have thrown up. His medications made him nauseous, and I was desperate to get him to eat.

They gave him three cartons of Kid Essentials Boost drink a day to help ease the number of food calories I had to pump into him, and he had to remain on these drinks for a year after his accident to prevent weight loss.

In addition to his pain and anxiety medications, he was taking nine other prescriptions that needed to be administered every two to six hours, depending on what they were. So, from the moment I woke up, I had to begin my medication charting or I would lose track of what needed to be taken and when. I had to take into account when he had eaten, as some had to be taken with a meal while others were given on an empty stomach. Not an hour went by when I didn't have to give him some drug or treatment.

Every few hours I would take his blood pressure and chart his numbers so the research department could track to see how well his heart medications were working.

After breakfast we would attend each appointment. When there were breaks between appointments, we would go up to the playroom where Fulton would become a little child again. Dinosaurs and trucks, and even a tricycle were waiting for him. He loved going there.

Then it was back to the Ronald McDonald House for a quick nap, but only if his medication schedule allowed.

We then returned to the hospital for physical therapy, which lasted two to three hours a day. It was painful and exhausting, and I was struck early on how much strength and coordination Fulton had lost during his hospital stay and all that was required to stretch his tendons, which had shrunk from disuse. He had to regain his balance and learn to navigate around corners without bumping into walls. He could not hop, skip, or jump, or even raise his arms above his head. Therapy was made to be as much fun as possible, but I could see how much it took out of him every day.

We always ended his physical therapy appointments with scar massage therapy which may sound pleasant and relaxing, but it was really quite painful for him. His scars were quickly becoming thick and lumpy. Hours of daily massaging are required to help break up the fibers that form beneath the grafted skin. The worst for him were the mouth massages. The scars surrounding his mouth prevented him from being able to open his mouth. Feeding time required him to use straws and tiny forks and spoons. When he was not eating, he had to wear mouth stretchers to prevent his mouth from contracting further. Unfortunately the scars around his mouth healed in such a way that his lower lip curled completely outward and fused to his chin, exposing the inner membranes of his mouth. So, while his lips were not actually burned, due to him sucking them in while on fire, he will still need extensive surgeries around his mouth to maintain his ability to open his mouth up wide enough to eat and eventually correct his lower lip.

He was fitted with custom pressure garments, which restricted extensive capillary development within the scars and helped lessen how puffy the scars became. These garments had to be replaced every three months for the first year, and every six months after that, until he was finally released from having to wear them at all. What a happy day that was!

Fulton was blessedly spared from having many of his major joints burned. These types of burns can severely restrict movement and would have required a lot of extra therapy, and I am fully aware of how blessed he was to not have been burned more than he was.

His facial scars were our biggest concern, as he was unable to wear a pressure mask like most burn patients would. Fulton developed large sores on his head that absolutely refused to heal on their own. By the end of March we were so desperate to have them heal, the surgeons agreed to actually perform skin grafts on these spots to make sure he was completely covered when they sent us home. Unfortunately, the sores broke through even the grafted skin, and we continued to struggle with this painful affliction until the end of October 2013, when all at once they decided to close on their own.

All testing for infections came back negative, and the doctors were stumped as to what these wounds could be. In desperation I began studying herbal healing methods and actually found a lot of helpful treatments for him. Even the hospital's research department began to take notice, and last I heard at least a few doctors said they wanted to learn more about the benefits of calendula on healing skin. Fulton still has occasional outbreaks a few days after he has follow up skin grafts, so we believe it must be some sort of autoimmune reaction to the stress of the surgeries and have now learned to expect a round of intense washing and bandage changes twice a day like we did when we were still in Galveston. It is a good reminder of how far we have come, and a humbling reminder that there will be more suffering in Fulton's future until he receives his last surgeries when he is grown.

Soon after we were released to live in the Ronald McDonald House, we decided we needed to get Fulton into a more "homelike" environment to speed up his healing even more. While we were very grateful for the shelter the Ronald McDonald House provided, it was not the best overall environment for us. There were too many regulations in this particular house that directly affected and even restricted the care he required.

I had met a woman, Heather, a few weeks earlier, and with her help, we rented a house next to her home and immediately fell into a state of semi-normalcy. I had my own kitchen to cook the meals Fulton was used to eating before the accident, which helped him gain weight. And I could perform all the medical care Fulton needed without worry. It was still quite stressful overall, but dare I say we actually enjoyed some of the time we spent there.

Yes, the house was a tremendous financial drain, as we stayed there for two months, but the emotional oasis it provided brought about quicker healing in the long run. Was it a selfish move? Perhaps. But I was truly at a breaking point and came to realize that there are times to embrace the mortification opportunities and times to find temporal relief where I could. I feel that as long as I accept the crosses I have been given, I do not think Our Lord minds when I find ways of adjusting smaller crosses to make them more bearable.

The remainder of our stay in Galveston had many peaks and valleys, but overall we were healing. I say 'we' because aside from the initial trauma of the day of the accident, the emotional toll of taking on the brunt of his care on my own was exhausting. Those months of being the one to have to inflict such pain on him several times a day have changed me as a parent. And those days are still not over, as Fulton still requires several surgeries a year.

While Jay is always more than willing to take over with Fulton's aftercare, I seemed to have developed a sense of responsibility and ownership of his post-surgical care. I know him in ways no one else does. We are a team, and I love helping him heal. This, for me, has become a form of therapy. Being so closely involved in his ongoing care reminds me of how far we have come, how far we have yet to go, and how close Our Lord has kept us every step of the way.

***

Your ways are indeed not mine, O Lord, as I know I would have chosen the easy way out. But I thank You in Your great wisdom for allowing me to participate in Fulton's care in such a way that I slowly learned to die to self. Those were difficult days, but they were days filled with much learning and many graces, and I thank You for every moment. Through the joys and tears, You remained by my side, strengthening me in my new role as nurse to my son. Please continue to guide me as Fulton requires continued care, and be generous with Your graces to all parents who so lovingly tend to their children's needs, no matter how tiring it may be. Amen.

CHAPTER 12

"Trust in the Lord with all your heart, and lean not on your own understanding; in all your ways acknowledge Him, and He shall direct your paths."
—*Proverbs 3:5-6*

Three months after the accident, a miraculously short time I have been told, Fulton was finally discharged from the hospital. We were headed home! It was exhilarating. Terrifying. Much more healing still had to take place, and unknown crosses still awaited us down the road, but we rejoiced as we finally reached this major milestone on our journey.

And what a journey it has been. I often reflect on how I felt that homecoming day. I reviewed our journey in amazement, the following thoughts going through my mind.

When we were minutes away from home after our two day drive home, I took this picture.

And one year later I wrote the following reflection:

Do you recognize this highway?

Probably not. Not at first, anyway. But I think we all have traveled on it—or one like it—in our lives. It is the path of life. Our highway to Heaven. Or to Hell.

I have traveled this road many times. It is the road we live on. There is nothing spectacular about it, really, beyond the fact that last year, at precisely the time I am writing this post today, I was on this road headed home. I hadn't been on this road for three months, and while it may look rather bland and uninteresting to you, it was profoundly beautiful to me. Heavenbound.

Three months before this photo was taken, on January 8, 2013, I had traveled this road with Fulton in the opposite direction, feeling as though I was headed into the flames of Hell. Riding shotgun in an ambulance, we headed to a nearby elementary school where a medical helicopter awaited to take my son to the hospital in Tulsa, OK. I remember very little of the ride. Just the prayers. And the one stop we had to make because they could not keep Fulton stabilized as we bumped along the road.

"Jesus, I trust in You. Mother Mary, help us." Over and over these prayers rose from my heart and streamed down my face. "Jesus, I trust in You. Mother Mary, help us."

Finally we arrived at the school, most likely ruining recess, and I anxiously waited while they tried to get my son stable enough for the 28 minute helicopter ride. "Where are we going?" Hell. This has got to be Hell.

"We are taking Fulton to Tulsa."

"You cannot go with."

"You will have to find another way and meet him there."

"The pilot never takes extras. We are so sorry."

Darkness.

Would he even be alive when I finally got there? Tulsa was over 2 hours away. What if he didn't make it? He would be all alone . . .

Lost.

I shivered in the January breeze and prayed.

And then, "The pilot says you may go! He has never let anyone ride along before!"

Praise God! Our first miracle!

Indeed the first two weeks were a spiritual agony—a hell of sorts—the worst times of our lives. But soon there were glimmers of hope. Over the course of the next few months, Fulton and I stayed the course, keeping our eyes on the ultimate prize: Home. Every day, every moment was dedicated towards the day we would return home.

There were speed bumps. There were detours. And a few times we feared the end was near. But by completely trusting in Our Lord, I knew that someday, somehow, we would be coming home again. I did not question. I did not force my will. I became like soft clay in the holy hands of Our Lord, and He shaped me, strengthened me and set me on the path I needed to be on to get us Home. For during that time, I had renewed my faith, grown closer to Our Lord and Our Lady and learned to embrace each cross with which I was blessed. God had a plan—not just for me, but for Fulton and my entire family. And I trusted Him completely. But, with my husband's help, it would be up to me to help guide my children through it.

Then finally, the day for which I both prayed and dreaded had come. The surgeons gathered around Fulton and I and unanimously agreed that it was indeed time to go home. We were ready. We were strengthened by their care and armed with what we needed. Not only the medical supplies and medications, but more importantly the prayers and continued support from all those around the world who followed on us on our journey. Without you all, I truly believe we would not have come through as well as we did. And I am so very grateful.

It was a journey—an adventure of sorts—not knowing where it would lead, but knowing that as long as I stayed faithful to the path that was set before me, it would all be right in the end. For strength, I feasted on the fruits that grew alongside the road—the struggles and miracles—the bitter and the sweet—and my eyes opened to the power that comes from completely surrendering to the will of God. Letting Him lead me where He willed, and slowly becoming the kind of wife, mother and woman I never would have become, had this road not been set before me. A path to holiness. A highway to Heaven.

Sure, I stumbled more than a few times while I was so far from home. There are many things I wish I had done differently if given the chance. But even through my failures I have learned how to better respond to the crosses and graces set before me in everyday life, and find ways of giving God the glory He so rightly deserves in all things. Hindsight is sometimes the best lens through which we try to see how to better respond. And I pray that I am able to apply what I have learned to whatever future roads Our Lord places before me.

As I look at the picture I took of our road, I recall how I felt as we traveled those last few miles: Excitement. Apprehension. Joy. And I see how, even after returning to our happy home filled with cake, balloons, and streamers, and after our new "real life" settled in, I am still on a journey. Firmly set on the pathway to holiness as wife and mother, guiding all my children as they embark on their own journeys, as they stumble along the roads He has set before each of them.

None of us have made it yet. But by the grace of God, one day, we will finally make it Home.

***

As each new day dawns, I thank You Lord for allowing me just one more day to complete my Heavenly quest. My final destination is clear, but the road remains hidden. Only You know what lies before me, and the pitfalls and helps that I may encounter along the way. Keep me ever focused on the ultimate goal and may I continue to be in awe of the many ways You have gently guided me on this journey. Continue to bless me with the trials and consolations my soul requires that I may one day arrive, gratefully, at Your gates and at Your feet. Amen.

Jay and Cassandra on their wedding day 1995.

One of the last photos taken of Fulton before his accident.

Christmas before the accident. Upon returning home from Midnight Mass, Fulton found the Christmas tree surrounded by presents, and the Infant Jesus in His manger. He was fascinated with the Infant Jesus and could not be distracted from the manger.

A typical breakfast for Fulton — 5 liquid medications plus one crushed pill in yogurt.

Fulton was finally allowed to go on an outing away from the hospital. We took a ferry ride and watched the dolphins swim alongside the boat.

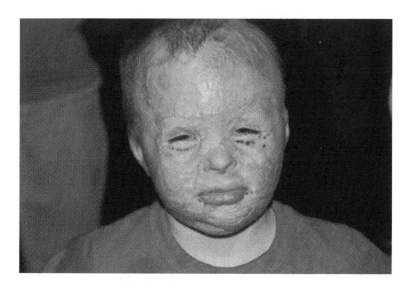

Homecoming! This photo was taken as his siblings welcomed him home at last.

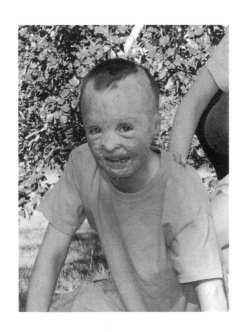

A very happy, healthy boy!

All of the Poppe children – 2016

SECTION 2:

Lessons Learned

CHAPTER 13

"You are like a block of marble in the hands of the sculptor.
The sculptor must chip, hew and smooth it to make it into a
statue that is a work of art. God wishes to make us the living
image of Himself. All we need to think of is to keep still in His
hands while He works on us, and we can rest assured that the
chisel will never strike the slightest blow that is not needed for
His purposes and our sanctification; for, as St. Paul says,
the will of God is your sanctification."
— Father Jean Baptiste Saint-Jure

How do we make sense of such events, where pain and suffering are so immense? We easily become overwhelmed at the prospect of pain or loss and shy away from anything uncomfortable. The temptation is to cry out to God in anger, demanding that He tell us why such things could happen. But such ranting is useless, for we would scarcely understand His answers if He were to tell us. It would be too difficult to comprehend when the wounds are still so fresh. Dare I say His reasons, if revealed so early on, could very well drive us away from Him if He revealed His plan before we were ready.

Early on in my conversion, St Louis de Montfort took me under his wing and gave to me a deeper understanding of the power behind the rosary and the changes that can occur in a person's heart with Our Lady's guidance. Mary's sole purpose is to bring souls to her Son, which she does by gently taking us through the Gospels, showing us the virtues we must perfect within us, that we too may be perfect as our Heavenly Father is perfect. Her virtues truly are the treasures hidden within the rosary, and once I found them I couldn't let them go.

I returned to the first Joyful Mystery, the Annunciation, time and time again at the hospital. This mystery is prayed for humility—the cornerstone of all other virtue. And within humility must come a complete surrender to Our Lord's will, no matter what His will may be.

Picture, if you will, Our Lady in the Annunciation. Quietly at prayer in the privacy of her room, she is suddenly visited by an angel, bestowing upon her the highest honor and presenting to her a most precious request.

"Hail Mary, full of grace . . ." Hail Mary? Only royalty in her culture were addressed with the word 'hail,' and in her humility, she was troubled by this greeting. The angel then proceeded to tell her of God's great plan for her and for the world: would she accept His request?

Mary's humility within this mystery is so beautifully expressed. Her plans for her life, no doubt, did not include becoming the mother of God. Her vow of virginity had already been accepted by God, and she was concerned how she was to become a mother without breaking her vow. *How could this be?* she pondered. But God works in mysterious ways, and the angel reassured her that her vow would be honored and God's will fulfilled.

Mary's unconditional fiat is the perfect model for us whenever Our Lord allows a change in our life. These changes are usually not foreseen. We have our future planned, imagining how we will live the rest of our days. But when the life we had envisioned is taken from us, through an accident, grave persecution, an unexpected death or disease, how should we respond?

"Let it be done to me according to Your word."

This may be difficult to hear, especially when the cross you carry is so heavy. But know that, in allowing suffering to come to you, the all-loving and all-merciful God has your best interests at heart. Resisting His loving hand and His invitation as you shoulder your cross will make your cross unbearable. Bitterness and anger will weigh you down, separating yourself from Him and blocking the graces with which He was prepared to bless you.

The suffering we experience in life is rooted in our fallen nature. Before the Crucifixion, suffering had no meaning. But Jesus' sacrificial suffering transformed meaningless misery into an opportunity to offer Him acts of love and mortification for the benefit of our own souls and the souls of others. By accepting your suffering as a powerful means of sanctification, your suffering suddenly has purpose. And your load becomes light, for "My yoke is sweet and my burden light" (Matt. 11:30). You are released from the pressure of performing bravely, alone. Instead you are enveloped in His love, with Our Blessed Mother as your guide, drawing from her example the faith required to embrace His will in all things and ultimately transforming your pain into glory.

St. Paul of the Cross tells us "In uniting yourself to God's will, you take on new life and gather great courage, willingly embracing the cross and kissing His hand even when it chastises you, a hand that reaches out to you in love and has no other intention but your greater spiritual well-being."

As I mentioned in my conversion story, one year before Fulton's accident I read the book A Trustful Surrender to Divine Providence by Father Jean Baptiste Saint Jure, S.J. and Saint Claude de la Colombiere, S.J. This tiny book, available in the public domain, proved to be a powerhouse of meditations and is structured so that one can easily use it for daily reading and meditation.

God has not revealed His entire nature to us, but we can trust that by what He has chosen to reveal, He always wills for us to be saved. Not a single soul has been created for damnation. And it is by perfect conformity to His will that we are to grow in holiness.

But sometimes, when the burden is so heavy we can hardly face the day, we struggle to accept His loving hand in the events unfolding before us. At times it was only through gritted teeth I could say "You allowed this, O Lord. Thy will be done" as I wrestled with the urge to run. I simply had to trust He desired that a greater good would come of the pain, and I persevered.

If we are struggling to accept the love behind our current crosses, how do we go about embracing the cross He allowed to come to us? Sometimes looking to an all-powerful God seated on His throne in Heaven can make some souls timid, or even angry. "Why are You not fixing this?" some cry out. Or "How could You allow this to happen?"

If you struggle with these barriers, trust in the good words of St. Paul of the Cross: "I wish that all men could understand the great favor that God grants them when, in His goodness, He (allows) them suffering . . . for then the soul, like gold which is purified in the fiery crucible, is cleansed, made beautiful, detached from earthly things, and united to the Sovereign Good, without even being conscious of it."

Taking that leap of faith and saying "yes" to God's will could be considered an act of heroic virtue. It is extremely difficult to accept that which causes such pain. It is even more difficult to say in your heart that such suffering could actually be ultimately viewed as a blessing.

Sometimes surviving the day without giving up is a glory to God who will sustain us in all difficulties, if only we let Him. It is not for us to say in what form God's glory will be made manifest. It is simply our duty to suffer well, and remain open to how we are to participate, trusting we will be guided to do what He wills through it all.

For those who are hurting, I know that this message may not be fully understood right now. And that is OK. I have learned that either a soul has already been softened to embrace God's will, or it is a lesson learned in hindsight. And only rarely is such light able to penetrate a heart that is in the throes of suffering. Just keep your heart open to Him. Meditate frequently on the Sorrowful Mysteries. On Our Lord's gift of suffering to the world. On Our Lady's fiat at the foot of the Cross. Your suffering will find a home within one of these safe havens and it is there that God will be glorified through you. And peace will eventually come.

**

Act of Abandonment
By Saint Francis De Sales

O my God, I thank you and I praise you for accomplishing your holy and all-lovable will without any regard for mine. With my whole heart, in spite of my heart, do I receive this cross I feared so much!
It is the cross of Your choice, the cross of Your love. I venerate it; nor for anything in the world would I wish that it had not come, since You willed it.
I keep it with gratitude and with joy, as I do everything that comes from Your hand; and I shall strive to carry it without letting it drag, with all the respect and all the affection which Your works deserve. Amen.

CHAPTER 14

"Let us understand that God is a physician, and that suffering
is a medicine for salvation, not a punishment for damnation."
—*St. Augustine*

Those first days were filled with pain and prayer. So many things were happening, there was not much time to take a step back and let it all sink in. But at night, the silence allowed the question "why" to creep into my heart. I knew by now that the resignation to God's will was the only way to survive this tragedy. Yet I could not resist entertaining the urge to place blame. I could not blame God. No, that did not feel right. But was I perhaps the one to blame?

The only thing protecting me from completely blaming myself was the fact that I was not near Fulton when it happened. I was right where I was supposed to be and could not for the life of me figure out what my role in his accident must be. My old feelings of pride and control took over and insisted that I would have somehow seen what was going to happen and called out a warning. Yes, if only I were outside at the time to do so.

I realized early on that this temptation was a coping mechanism, helping me to regain a sense of control. By blaming myself, it offered some semblance of control, helping to make sense of the accident. Being able to at least explain how the suffering began offered a little comfort, even if I did not yet fully know the reason why it happened to begin with.

Below is a blogpost I wrote, exploring a little of the whys involved in Fulton's accident, as I desperately grasped at straws to make sense of it all. The entry is a little theologically imperfect and looking back I see its flaws, but bear with me as I discuss it further below.

"I write this from the bedside of my son, Fulton, for whom all of you have been praying. Innocent child, arms in splints stretched out to either side of him, face thoroughly burned but with recognizable traits that are Fulton's alone. My son lies here on his bed, and I at his feet, and I am deeply sorrowful. But I am also profoundly grateful for this Cross that has come to me.

It may sound strange at first to think a mother could be grateful for such a tragedy, especially while his wounds are still so fresh. So, please allow me to explain.

I am a selfish, slothful woman, prone to all sorts of self-centered thoughts and actions. Not a day has gone by since my conversion that, after my examination of conscience, I have not realized at least some of my countless acts of pride and self-centeredness. I am a wounded woman, only beginning to see my own wretchedness and wanting to make amends any way I can.

Whenever I went through the day without prayer and without my spiritual compass, I unconsciously directed my actions and the actions of those around me to circle around my needs, my moods, and my whims. By day's end, everyone was grumpy (including me!) and not much was accomplished within my home and certainly nothing was done for love of God.

I prayed fervently for Our Lord to teach me how to die to self, to keep me from falling into those moments when my heart longs for that which is pleasing, comfortable, and easy. Too much time on the computer, snacking without thought between meals, working on unnecessary projects by myself instead of interacting with my children—all of these things kept my heart and energy focused on self instead of on others and on God.

Apparently I needed more than a few whispered words of encouragement to get me on the narrow path. I needed an intervention. And not just the kind where your friends take you out to lunch and express their concerns. I am talking about a real hard, "smack on the side of the head with a two by four" kind of intervention. One I could not dismiss and one that demanded more than a half-hearted attempt to get my act together. And on January 8, that two by four along with a burning barrel full of scraps of wood and a can of gasoline, exploded and changed my life forever.

Our home is loving, happy, and fairly clean most of the time. I feed my family well and have on many occasions been called "mean" because of my decisions to protect my children's bodies and souls. My children know and love their faith, and as far as I know, everyone who knows us enjoys my family's company. We have our faults and have had our dark moments, but on the whole, we are a healthy, thriving family, and no one has any reason to believe otherwise. I myself thought we were doing pretty well.

But God sees my private moments, those times when I would rather bury myself in a book than teach a child how to read one. Or when I dove into worldly hobbies or distractions instead of meeting the demands of a homesteading family of eight. Or the times when chatting with people I never even met in real life was more important than chatting with my children about their day. And it was precisely because of these moments that He decided to take my prayers for the grace to die to self to heart and answer them as He saw fit. And it is humbling to realize what a train wreck I must be in the eyes of God, to see that it would take such a dramatic event to begin to truly convert my heart.

Despite all of that, I am not feeling guilty, brooding in self-pity, or slipping into despair. Instead, I am energized at the challenge put before me. Fulton is healing each day, and with each passing day, my role in his care increases. Soon, and for many years after, I will be the one giving him the special burn baths, counting every single calorie that goes into his body, and forcing him to eat two and a half times the caloric amount he previously consumed, administering all medications, taking his heart rate and blood pressure multiple times a day, giving him scar massages, working with him two or more hours a day in physical therapy, and holding him close to my heart when he cries with exhaustion and pain, and encouraging him to keep on going.

Praise God, there is no room for self-love in this schedule! I am sure my weak nature will find time to grab for myself, but as long as I use it to fill my soul with the strength to go on, even my occasional time out with a book or an extra granola bar can be used to help me persevere and dive back into caring for my little boy, the object of my love, my source of sanctification.

I have resigned myself to accept this answered prayer and trust that with God's grace I will overcome myself and finally learn to love Him as He wants to be loved. Our Sorrowful Mother has already taught me so much—that the suffering of the innocent can, in His great design, bring about much good for many souls and will refine one's love for Him in ways previously unimaginable. I will attempt to linger at her side, watching her as she teaches me how to minister at the foot of the Cross placed before me, and pray I remain loyal to this calling."

I truly believed my need for further refinement was the direct cause of Fulton's accident and it was indeed my fault. I realize now that God simply permitted the accident to happen, ultimately intending for my entire family to be refined by fire. God did not rub His hands in glee as Fulton burned. Perhaps Fulton's Guardian Angel even wept. But once the explosion occurred, His plan for my family was set in motion and it was up to us to respond appropriately.

The Church does not teach that all illness or accidents are a direct result of past sins. Forgiveness is freely offered to the repentant soul who contritely confesses his sins and does penance. And while we most certainly have sinful tendencies and residual temporal punishment we have yet to atone for in our lives, the trials and tribulations that come our way are not in and of themselves punishments. They are, instead, opportunities to grow in love for the Lord and ultimately perfect our souls.

One of our F.S.S.P. priests once said in his homily that all things are either the will of God or permitted by God. Some may take offense to this and rage against the One who loves us most, but I take great comfort in this fact. He went on to explain that when such tragedies arise, He watches our patience and endurance and anxiously awaits the repentance of sinners. Whether the sinner is the person going through the trials or a soul across the ocean does not matter. Somehow, somewhere, souls are returning to Our Lord through our suffering. The redemptive suffering of the Passion continues, in part, through us and our willingness to suffer well for God's glory.

***

Lord, help us use our time of suffering to perfect the defects Our Lord has seen within us, and praise Him for allowing us this chance to give Him our fiat. May we offer to Him our life to do with it as He pleases, and offer to Him our will, that it be perfectly conformed to His and know we will be greatly blessed for this ultimate sacrifice. Amen.

CHAPTER 15

*"How often in these situations must Mary have returned
inwardly to the hour when God's angel had spoken to her,
pondering afresh the greeting: 'Rejoice, full of grace!'
and the consoling words: 'Do not be afraid!' The angel
departs; her mission remains, and with it matures her inner
closeness to God, a closeness that in her heart she is
able to see and touch."*
—Pope Benedict XVI

Oftentimes, when we were still in the hospital, the suffering was
too much for my heart to bear. Day after day of feeling helpless,
watching more and more tissue die off, watching the monitors
show numbers that he was headed downward instead of healing,
arms aching to cradle him, but only allowed to touch his toes
peeking out from the thick Ace bandages and braces on his leg.
*Mother Mary, was this what it was like for you as you watched your Son on
the Cross?* I imagined her at Jesus' feet, unable to comfort Him
with her caress but only able to reach above her to touch His
foot. My own heart was bursting, yet I knew she suffered so
much more than I.

Then suddenly one day, more than anything I craved the
sacred. My eyes were starving for something beyond the temporal
suffering that lay before me. I needed desperately to go to Mass,
to help properly understand everything I was feeling and
experiencing. I knew God's will was at work. I trusted Him
completely. But just as Fulton needed me to touch his toes and

whisper consoling words to him, so I needed the consoling word of God and to feel His presence. I needed to be close to Him, if only for a moment.

The weather was gray and chilly, and a fine mist settled around me as I walked the several blocks to Sunday Mass. I remember nothing about the sights I saw, only the prayers that filled my heart as I journeyed to His house. *Sweet Mary, my Mother, accompany me this morning. Open my heart to the lessons you want to teach me this day. Show me how to bear the swords that pierce my heart. Hail Mary . . .*

The church itself was pure white stone on the inside, a perfect complement to the beach town atmosphere of Galveston. I knelt in exhausted adoration in the pew, hardly conscious of my unusual posture compared to those around me. There was nothing left within me, unable to either stand or sit, and so I simply knelt and listened. The Gospel began.

"A reading from the Gospel of John Chapter 2 . . ." the priest began. "And the third day, there was a marriage in Cana of Galilee: and the mother of Jesus was there . . . And Jesus also was invited, and his disciples, to the marriage." (John 2:1-2)

When this Gospel began, I was taken back to an earlier time in my conversion when I struggled mightily with the Catholic devotions to Our Blessed Mother. I had still harbored the Protestant view of Mary long after I had been convicted of other Catholic doctrine. And one day, willing to learn whatever it was Mary wanted to teach me, I opened the bible to this particular Gospel. I was using my mother's older bible that day, though, and the language was a little strange to me, but as I read it, it became clear to me what I was to learn.

"And the wine failing, the mother of Jesus saith to him: They have no wine. And Jesus saith to her: Woman, what is that to me and to thee? my hour is not yet come. His mother saith to the waiters: Whatsoever he shall say to you, do ye." (John 2:3-5)

I already understood the beautiful and deeply theological significance of Jesus calling His mother "woman." But what about the "to Me and to thee"? This was something new. Most modern translations have eliminated the "and to thee" part of the original text and I wondered what it meant. It turned out, after consulting a priest, that Our Lord was not rebuking His mother as so many people think, but instead was asking her if she was prepared to accept all that would occur if He should perform this first public miracle. He asked her, in essence, for her second fiat, to allow Him to take His first step towards Calvary. And without hesitating to take her own heart into account, Our Blessed Mother turns to the servants and tells them to do as Our Lord commands.

Mother and Son, bound together, each carrying a cross designed for them, and each accepting fully God's will and the suffering that comes with it.

The wedding feast at Cana not only opened my eyes, but opened my heart to Mary in the most beautiful way that day and it has since become one of my most cherished Gospel stories. A constant reminder of accepting God's will, no matter what the cost, and allowing Him to work His wonders without me hindering His greater plans. As Mary gave her fiat at the wedding, her assent to suffering for the greater glory of God, so I too gave my complete fiat to Our Lord to do as He willed with Fulton and my family that morning at Mass.

Suffering has already come to us, O Lord. Please sanctify it. Transform this suffering into abundant graces. Just as Our Blessed Mother accepted the suffering that would come to her heart, I too give You my assent. And just as she immediately turned outward toward others to help them in their need, I ask for the graces to imitate her holy example and remain focused on the needs of others as well. Let no amount of suffering be wasted, but draw from it all I have to give to be used as You see fit. All glory to God.

It was an exhausting fiat, yet freeing at the same time, and I felt the changes almost immediately. What was before an inward acceptance and compliance to God's holy will and patient waiting for His plans to be revealed became fire within my heart to actively seek those who needed spiritual wine. I said to Him, "They have no wine," to which He reminded me that prayers combined with an acceptance of suffering were most powerful. And without knowing the cost, I always said yes. I knew my heart was to undergo pain as it had never before experienced. But I also knew Our Lady would not leave me alone in my agony. She would forever put before me the image of her remaining steadfast yet sorrowful at Our Lord's feet, lifting Him up to God, trusting that her suffering when joined with His would save countless souls. *Our Sorrowful Mother, help me be like you.*

As I headed back to the hospital, I prayed that my heart remain steadfast in my mission. *Holy Ghost, give to me the gift of perseverance, for You know how weak I am. Enflame in me a great love for Our Lord, that I willingly offer Him my ongoing fiat, accepting all that comes our way as Your holy will and a powerful means of conversion for myself, for Fulton and for all those in need of conversion. Show to me the souls who long for You, and teach me how to bring Your light to them in little ways. Please use my prayers, works and sufferings for this end or for whatever Your will desires. My Lord and my All, I give it all to You.*

***

Mary, most holy Virgin and Queen of Martyrs, accept the sincere homage of my filial affection. Into thy Heart, pierced by so many swords, do thou welcome my poor soul. Receive it as the companion of thy sorrows at the foot of the Cross, on which Jesus died for the redemption of the world. With thee, O sorrowful Virgin, I will gladly suffer all the trials, contradictions, and infirmities which it shall please Our Lord to send me. I offer them all to thee in memory of thy sorrows, so that every thought of my mind and every beat of my heart may be an act of compassion and of love for thee. And do thou, sweet Mother, have pity on me, reconcile me to thy Divine Son, Jesus; keep me in His grace and assist me in my last agony, so that I may be able to meet thee in Heaven and sing thy glories.

Most holy Virgin and Mother, whose soul was pierced by a sword of sorrow in the Passion of thy Divine Son, and who in His glorious Resurrection was filled with never-ending joy at His triumph, obtain for us who call upon thee, so to be partakers in the adversities of Holy Church and the Sorrows of the Sovereign Pontiff, as to be found worthy to rejoice with them in the consolations for which we pray, in the charity and peace of the same Christ our Lord. Amen.
—Traditional prayer

CHAPTER 16

"What does love look like? It has the hands to help others. It has the feet to hasten to the poor and needy. It has eyes to see misery and want. It has the ears to hear the sighs and sorrows of men. That is what love looks like."
—*St. Augustine of Hippo*

One cannot remain in crisis mode for long. Eventually a person must decide whether they are going to shoulder the cross with which they have been blessed or become a cross for another. When the whirlwind is still spinning and nothing has settled, I believe we as human beings are entitled to our rants and occasional tantrums. But acceptance and its resulting peace should be our ultimate goal.

We will not do this perfectly. We cannot. Human nature, being as it is, can easily take over when our hearts are weary, causing us to stumble as we carry our cross. Do not become discouraged when you fail in this task. Keep trying, to be sure, but when you stumble, raise your eyes from the dusty ground and search for those God has sent to help you stand again. They will be there. Maybe not in a way you hoped or even expected, but they will be there.

It is not by chance St. Louis de Montfort encourages us to meditate on patience when we pray the fourth Sorrowful Mystery. We live in unfortunate times, where patience it would seem is no longer needed. A trip to California from New York used to take months to complete via horseback or covered wagon. And if you made it, chances are you buried a few family members along the way, and you were grateful for completing the journey. Today, the same trip takes a few hours, yet we complain about the service, the lost piece of luggage or a crying baby sitting two rows away. And when we arrive at our destination, we are more than ready to unload our complaints to our friends or relatives who were anxiously awaiting our arrival.

Meals are cooked so fast, all we have to do is state our desires into a little metal box, drive a few feet away and get handed a bag of the very food we ordered. Yet we complain if the fries are not hot enough or the cheese slipped off the burger.

We get antsy if we have to wait too long in line to purchase a basketful of food that would have taken months to grow. The absolute miracle of the United States Postal Service is all but lost on us as we get annoyed if a letter is delivered a little slower than expected. And I have listened to more than enough rants about people who were too slow to return a phone call or answer a text.

We demand the best possible outcomes for the least amount of effort. And we have come to expect the best possible quality for the least amount of expense. Just stand in line at the customer service desk in Walmart as one after another bewildered customer bemoans the failure of some miscellaneous, poor quality, Made in China product.

When we as a culture have been so trained towards a life of entitlement and leisure, is it any wonder so few are truly equipped to carry the heavy burdens Our Lord asks us to bear?

When tragedy strikes, He weeps when so many run to a lawyer before running to Him. We seek justice. Compensation. Our pride appeased or our difficulties lifted. But how many seek meekness? Rouse their hearts to contrition? Or strive for wisdom or humility?

Our lives of comfort have created within us a detestation of suffering of any sort. A headache is treated with a pill, or a heartache with a drink. And when we have grown so weak in our ability to suffer even the smallest pains, what happens when our suffering multiplies? We lose patience. And with it we lose our sense of joy found within our suffering.

I invite you instead to take the slow, back roads to Calvary, appreciating the cuts and the scrapes we get along the way as a sign that we are still living and are loved by God so much that He is giving us the time we need to better prepare ourselves for Eternity. Bathe another's wound as Our Lady would have washed Our Lord's sacred wounds. Relish the freedom you feel when you truly forgive someone for an accident they caused, and embrace them to help alleviate their pain. Be grateful for the little blessings that come to you after a large loss and take the time to appreciate these smaller things in life that mean so much.

Strive to truly smell the roses growing alongside your road to Calvary. Our Lord did as much. As he walked, He loved. He saw the hearts of every single person jeering at Him as He struggled with His Cross. And He loved. This very love for those who added to His Cross is what kept Him moving forward, that He may carry His Cross and ultimately die for them, that they may live.

How can we imitate such patience? It truly is as easy as "offering it up"! Begin in small ways. Say your morning offering from the heart as best you can and let the day begin. Your first intention of the day was to make an offering to Our Lord. He will take that intention and even if you forget to patiently carry your cross the rest of the day, all will not be lost.

Pray for a patient and mortified heart. I learned early on how alleviating someone else's burdens helped alleviate my own. Especially when the giving hurts, just a little. Give a grieving widow your favorite heirloom rosary. Share your last meal with a hungry neighbor. Apply your sufferings to a holy soul in Purgatory.

I have learned that there are far more ways of alleviating other people's suffering than there are of alleviating your own. Mortify yourself, offer up prayers for others, accept God's will humbly in all things, and bear all things with love. By choosing to step out of yourself and generously reaching out to others, you will strengthen the virtues growing within you, giving you the inner peace and joy no million-dollar lawsuit could ever touch. Trying to lessen the weight of your own cross brings more pain to yourself both in this world and the next. Accept it all in the name of the Father who loves you and is leading you to happiness. Through this passion, all suffering becomes joy.

Throughout all the dramatic ups and downs we experienced, Our Lady always kept me at the foot of the cross. Countless consolations came to me in all forms—care packages sent by strangers, friendly visitors and home-cooked meals, hundreds of cards, letters, sacramentals, emails, and donations that allowed Jay to visit every two or three weeks. We were also blessed with new friends, some of whom still to this day remain dear to Fulton and our family. We were overwhelmed by the countless blessings sent our way.

The hospital, too, offered unlimited help to us both. They took care of my every need: food, clothing, and shelter, talks with the therapist on bad days, training classes on how to care for Fulton's wounds, and classes on physical therapy. This all-encompassing care gave me the confidence to be the nurse Fulton would eventually need me to be. The meticulous attention and respect they showed to me helped Fulton to thrive for the simple reason that I was made so comfortable there.

Those first few weeks in the hospital were exhausting for us both. So many tears, so many prayers, so much heartache. But through it all, the shadow of the cross consoled me and kept me focused on what truly mattered—a closer walk with God, converted hearts, and praise to God in all things.

As Fulton and I lived our own personal Passion each day, I prayed for a St. Veronica and St. Simon to come into my life. It was very lonely, and when things were at their worst, my only temporal consolation at night was a box of Kleenex and a pillow. No shoulder to cry on, no one to relieve me for an hour or two to keep watch over Fulton's bedside while I napped or simply took a walk on the beach.

There were many wonderful people who stopped by the hospital to offer freshly cooked meals for me and little gifts for Fulton, but being the incredibly shy person that I was, it was painfully difficult for me to be around strangers. It was an additional cross to bear, of sorts, and I stumbled more than a few times. But I was always so grateful to all who opened their hearts to us.

One of the first Veronicas appeared to me a few days after being in the hospital. A doctor came into the room bearing a beautiful gift basket with a card and books for Fulton. They came from his wife who had read about Fulton's accident on CatholicMom.com. She and her children put together the gift bag and sent it with the good doctor who worked at the UTMB hospital across the street. She and her friend frequently offered their time to help me run errands or simply provide a meal from time to time. And later, when Fulton and I were partially discharged but still required to live close to the hospital, they even brought me groceries. I sorely regret not getting to know these wonderful women better, as they reached out to me on many occasions. But timing was not on my side and I was unable to respond as I should have.

There were other people as well, a little girl who made me lunch, and others who introduced themselves to me or came bearing gifts. To all of you Veronicas, I thank you so very much! My mind and heart were so full of concern for Fulton, it left me little room for others at the time, and I failed to live up to the social graces I knew I should possess.

Even with the steady supply of Veronicas with whom I was coming into contact, I still needed a Simon to see me through.

Then one day, a Facebook message arrived, saying: "Cassandra, I am a friend of Julie's and she told me you were on the island. If you need anything at all, please do not hesitate to give me a call. I will be stopping by this evening with dinner . . ." Little did I know this woman was to be the answer to my prayers.

Heather was a woman about my age who lived a few blocks from the hospital. She brought a homemade meal and a picnic basket full of miscellaneous items to help bring me comfort. From holy water to mace, she had thought of everything. "I tossed in this picture of the Holy Family," she explained as she held up the framed picture. "I thought you would need something nice to look at, so I just grabbed this off my wall."

That was the kind of person she was. Generous beyond belief, and a heart open to taking on some of the suffering I was enduring. There was no pressure for me to talk, which was good, because small talk has always been painfully awkward for me. We ate some meals with only minimal words, and I was completely at ease with her. Later, as we became good friends, she and Fulton became close as well. She became my chauffeur when I needed to run an errand or just escape for awhile, my chef when I could not eat another bite of cafeteria food, my real estate agent when I was looking for a place to rent, and most importantly, my prayer warrior and my friend. Without Heather, I do not know how long I could have persevered. For even though I was resigned to God's will, I was stumbling under the weight of my shyness and loneliness. God sent me Heather to help me shoulder some of those weights. She was indeed my Simon.

As I so earnestly prayed for my own St. Veronicas and Simons in the beginning, I learned how to become a St. Veronica for others as well. Being the one giving instead of receiving was far easier for me to do, and I readily opened my heart to the other parents around me. Surrounded by my bountiful blessings, I passed on these blessings to other families. I offered words of encouragement to new families as their children were admitted. I fed patients' siblings the treats I received in the mail. I even offered to pay for a hotel room for a family member of a patient who did not qualify for the hospital's housing benefits. And of course, I prayed for them all.

There is so much suffering in a burn unit. Unspeakable suffering that never seems to end. I have had military medics come to me, saying no doctor wanted to stay in the burn units in military hospitals for long because the suffering was too much to take. It truly takes a special soul to tend to the wounds and to the heart of a burn patient. And when the wails of an inconsolable infant in the room next door bring your own heart to tears, all you can do is pray.

I learned that such suffering becomes empowering when I used my own passion and pain to help another. It gave me a sense of purpose, a concrete reason for the senseless suffering around me. And so, to ease both my own suffering and that of another, I tried to envelope in my own imperfect way those around me in my arms, my heart, and my prayers, that we all may rise together triumphant in the end.

***

I thank you, Lord, for the countless souls You have placed before me and taught me true compassion. Thank You for the never-ending supply of consolations, for never leaving me unaided, and for giving to me my Mother Mary as the perfect example of who I am called to become. Forgive me when I failed to comfort another, for in those times I also failed to give You comfort. Help me to see every opportunity You put before me for what it is—a chance to sanctify myself, a chance to change another's heart and a chance to give You glory. Amen.

CHAPTER 17

"What does the poor man do at the rich man's door, the sick man in the presence of his physician, the thirsty man at a limpid stream? What they do, I do before the Eucharistic God. I pray. I adore. I love."
—*St. Francis of Assisi*

Day after day, I lay my head at Fulton's feet, helpless. The level of excruciating agony Fulton endured cannot be adequately described, and I prayed for relief. Relief from his pain. Relief from the terror he felt. And relief for myself.

"Father, if thou wilt, remove this chalice from me," were the words I prayed daily. Just as Our Lord collapsed under the weight of His agony in the garden, the sheer weight of what was before me kept me firmly on my knees. Every morning, for those first moments as I walked into his room and saw the fresh suffering, I allowed myself to both embrace the maternal desire to take this pain from my son and the utterly human desire to be rid of the agony we felt. But I would always end the prayer with a complete resignation to accept with love anything Our Lord chose to send our way.

The Sorrowful Mysteries have always been my favorite mysteries to pray because they are so richly steeped in the humanity of Our Lord. It is what draws me to Him and gives me strength. Especially the Agony in the Garden. Blessed Catherine Emmerich describes in painful detail all that He experienced in the Garden of Gethsemane. He saw our sins. He saw His suffering. He also saw the hearts that would remain indifferent to His love. The very idea pulls my heart to Him in such remorse and humility, there are times I want to crawl to Him in the garden and weep at His feet as St. Mary Magdelene once did. But because I cannot do this literally, I simply learn from Him how to survive the agonies that come to me in life.

He suffered long in the garden, as did I. And as Our Lord asks the Heavenly Father to let the cup pass from Him, His final prayer was also my own: "but yet not my will, but thine be done." (Luke 22: 42) I found it rather empowering when I realized that it was not until Our Lord verbally expressed the resignation of His own will that the angel came to tend to His needs. Yes, His agony continued, but He was now able to persevere due to the spiritual graces that came to Him. How could I behave any differently? And how could I expect Fulton and me to endure the grueling weeks ahead without spiritual comfort and sustenance?

Knowing Fulton could easily take a turn for the worse, I quickly sought out the Sacraments. I was frantic to find a priest to come and administer whatever Sacraments might be available to him. One priest came and prayed over him, for which I was truly grateful, but it was not enough. I wanted Fulton fully armed for whatever battles he would have to face. Thankfully, a friend from our home parish contacted a local, retired priest who still had the faculties to administer Sacraments. "Send him, please! As soon as he can get here!" I exclaimed.

Within a few days, he arrived. We sat in the hallway, just inside the ICU doors and talked for awhile. He carried with Him the Blessed Sacrament and heard my confession. I then knelt under the bright white lights of the sterile ICU hallway and received My Strength.

This priest's own cross was great; he had great difficulty walking down the hallway to Fulton's room. A neighboring patient's father saw the good priest and begged him to bless his daughter as well. And so he went, one painful step at a time, quietly fanning the breath of God to all the children in the ICU.

We came to Fulton's bedside at last. Already tired from his walk, the sight of Fulton took his breath away. He immediately began praying as he prepared the holy oil. He said the words of an emergency Confirmation, but hesitated when it came time to bless his head. Fulton was untouchable. His forehead, still glistening with patches of cadaver skin and exposed hypodermis, could not receive the blessed oil he so desperately needed.

My heart sank. *What now, Lord? He is Yours. Please make this happen.* As I prayed this, beneath the layers of bandages, Fulton's perfect left foot twitched. His perfect skin on that foot soon glinted with hope and holy oil, the rite of Confirmation was complete, and Fulton Joseph Poppe was a fully enrolled member of the Church Militant.

Grateful for the additional spiritual weapons we now had, I felt we could face anything that came our way. Of course, the suffering continued, and my own visit to the Garden of Gethsemane lasted far longer than I could have imagined. But just as the angels administered to Jesus in the garden, Our Lord always came to me when I needed Him most.

Many weeks later, when Fulton was still under close daily hospital supervision but was discharged under my care, we were finally able to see the rest of our family. It was Lent, and one of the FSSP priests in Texas drove all the way to Galveston to join us for dinner and a family blessing.

We prepared for his coming with such joy. He warned us that he would have with him the Blessed Sacrament, but I was in full Martha mode and forgot to prepare myself and the house to receive Him like Mary. All too soon, the doorbell rang. My daughters and I quickly grabbed our veils and everyone greeted Father at the door.

"I have the Blessed Sacrament. Where shall I place Him?"

Dear Lord, I have not prepared for You properly! I panicked. Too late to greet Him at the door with candles, we did our best to find candles for the altar in the unfamiliar house. Father stood patiently in the foyer while Jay and Ryan moved small cabinet and prepared a proper place for Our Lord to reside. White dishtowel, two candles, a bowl with water and a spoon. Father had his Crucifix, oils and Our Lord. We were ready. Each family member privately confessed, and I did a general confession, reviewing all my sins over a lifetime, careful to recall not only my sins but to specifically name the underlying sinful tendencies that led me to each sin. He gently revealed to me where these hidden tendencies resided in my heart, drawing them out into the open for me to see and properly confess.

When Jay and I came to the Catholic faith, I had always taken confession very seriously. I did not hold anything back when I confessed, but I never really dug to the core of my sinful nature until that day. But this day was different. It was the difference between simply weeding a garden and taking a shovel and completely overturning the entire soil bed, seeing for the first time where the deeper roots of those weeds gathered their nourishment. Humbled and grateful, as he said the prayers of absolution over me, the weight of a lifetime of darkness was finally lifted.

We were all quiet during this time, either waiting to confess, or quietly meditating on what Father counseled. Afterward, Father blessed Fulton, prepared us all to receive Our Lord through prayer and counsel, then kneeling on the dining room floor, Our Savior came to us—on our tongues and into our hearts.

It was the most powerful Lenten exercise I have ever had. Touched by the tender care Our Lord showed us, my tears flowed freely, as I once again joyfully renewed my wish to offer Him my fiat.

I had my resurrection early that Lent, and I realized how Our Lord longs for us to turn to Him and uses all means available to strengthen us on our journey. He could not have completed His mission of redemption without a firm resolution to fulfill God's will as He prayed in the garden. Great graces come to those who hold nothing back from God. And so just as the angel came to Jesus in the garden to strengthen Him, so He comes to all of us to give us the great gifts of faith, hope, patience, and perseverance through His Sacraments.

**

Anima Christi
Soul of Christ, sanctify me
Body of Christ, save me
Blood of Christ, inebriate me
Water from Christ's side, wash me
Passion of Christ, strengthen me
O good Jesus, hear me
Within Thy wounds hide me
Suffer me not to be separated from Thee
From the malicious enemy defend me
In the hour of my death call me
And bid me come unto Thee
That I may praise Thee with Thy saints
and with Thy angels
Forever and ever
Amen

CHAPTER 18

"The strategy of our adversary can be compared to the tactics of a commander intent upon seizing and plundering a position he desires. The leader of an army will encamp, explore the fortifications and defenses of the fortress, and attack at the weakest point."
—*St. Ignatius of Loyola*

Whenever one is trying to grow in holiness, the darker forces take notice and will use every advantage it is given to tear these efforts apart. The physical exhaustion that so frequently accompanies stressful situations added to my intense emotional suffering left me raw and exposed. And ripe for the attack.

As I learned to suffer, I thanked God for preparing me beforehand to be prepared for the spiritual attacks that inevitably came my way. For a little over a week, I was asked "What exactly happened?" and honestly, I did not know. I know what I saw, smelled, and heard, but truthfully it was not much. So much happened so quickly after the explosion I never thought to ask what had really happened, so I just assumed my version was real. We had a burn barrel going. A can of gasoline exploded. Fulton got burned. Jay saved him. It was enough for me, as I assumed the gas can was simply left too close to the fire and the fumes ignited. The finer details did not really matter to me, and I focused my energies on helping Fulton heal.

But one evening, early on, I was talking to Jay on the phone before going to sleep after a particularly grueling day, and I finally asked him, "So, what exactly did happen?"

There was a pause. The room seemed to turn a slightly darker hue of dread, and the story came out at last.

Jay and Fulton were gathering sticks but they couldn't build the fire up hot enough to do what it had to do. Burning the insides of chickens, plus their feathers and skin, require a very hot fire or it will get fairly stinky the next day, so everything had to be burned quickly and thoroughly.

Jay needed a larger fire, so, he explained, "I squirted gasoline into the fire and the can exploded in my hands." The fumes immediately travelled up the spout and into the can, which caused the explosion. CJ was just coming out of the chicken house with the first bird in his arms and saw the mushroom cloud of flames reach almost 30 feet in the air, singeing the tips of the branches of the oak tree over Jay's head and sending balls of flame shooting out from all sides. Fulton was just coming up behind Jay with another handful of sticks and was hit directly in the face and chest with one of these fireballs.

Miraculously, Jay not only survived, but was uninjured, except for some singed hair and eyebrows, but the front of his flannel jacket was in flames. For him, all it took was a simple 'stop, drop and roll', and the flames were out. Meanwhile Fulton, engulfed in flames, had turned around and was blindly walking away from the burn barrel.

"Dad!" CJ called, stunned. "Fulton is on fire!" Jay had no idea Fulton was even near him when the explosion occurred. Adrenaline still racing through him, Jay ran to Fulton and tackled him to the ground, the flames smothered then reignited with every move they made. We suspect the injuries Jay sustained were the result of his attempts to smother the raging flames furiously consuming Fulton.

His words, "I squirted gasoline into the fire, and the can exploded in my hand," replayed in my head, as I tried to make sense of it all. *You did WHAT?!* my mind screamed. Verbally I repeatedly reassured Jay that it was an accident. I loved him. We would get through this. But inside I was seething.

After I hung up, I raged at the ceiling above me, silently. I shook uncontrollably, frightened at the fierceness of my feelings. Darkness closed in around me like a thick blanket. Praise God, I recognized these feelings for what they were: A violent temptation intending to divide and conquer. I had felt it once before, that fateful night I intended to tell Jay I wanted a divorce. Recognizing it as a spiritual attack, I hit my knees and prayed.

I prayed harder that night than I did on the day of the accident, for so much was at stake. Now, not only did I have Fulton's survival and healing on my mind, but our marriage, the well-being of all our children, and Jay's emotional healing—all of these hinged on how well I fought off the temptation that now brutally assaulted me from all angles.

And the demons knew right where to strike: I was the wife left to pick up the pieces of his poor choice. I was the mother whose beloved son was near death in a hospital bed two floors below. I was the mother separated from her other children, who were also greatly suffering. I was the weak woman, craving the comforts of home. I was the lonely woman with no one with whom to share my pains. I was the sinful soul, well trained in the arts of nurturing pride.

I was livid.

It was a wrestling match like none other and I fear that if so many people around the world were not already praying for us, I might have given the temptation an open door to make itself at home within me, allowing it to fester and eventually poison my heart. Our marriage had survived a similar dose of such toxins, but it took years for Our Lord and me to undo the damage to my heart.

No. Not again. Not ever.

I finally fell asleep, exhausted, and awoke the next morning eternally grateful for not saying anything to Jay the night before. His was a stupid decision, and one to which he freely admits. Not a day goes by when he sees sweet Fulton's face that he is not reminded of the pain his poor decision caused Fulton and our entire family. It is one thing to allow someone to forgive and forget your sins. However, it is another thing to be forgiven but still daily see the scars and damage you did. I know he wrestles inwardly, feeling as though his own Guardian Angel wrapped its wings protectively around him to quite literally spare his life, while Fulton's Angel seemed to take a step back and allowed him to burn. Whether this is what actually happened or not, it is an image that frequently haunts him.

Truly, I can go for months without even thinking about Jay's role in the accident. The only time I am reminded is when friendly strangers ask us about what happened. Jay, however, does not have that luxury.

Looking more asleep than awake and still feeling bruised from the previous night's battle, I made my way up to the cafeteria and sat at my usual table. I faced the window that should have been looking out over the ocean. I had yet to see it clearly, as most days were drizzling and foggy, and the only view I had was of the iron bars lining the outside edge of the balcony outside.

That morning, the fog was still there, of course, but I could see further than I ever had previously. I was beginning to understand. All I was called to do was to trust the path we were set upon, and even though I could not see where it was headed, all would be made clear in His good time. This journey was not to be about Fulton. It was not about me. Instead, it was to be about a family who will struggle with whatever this journey brings them and will have to choose daily to fall or to triumph over the snares set in our paths.

I then recalled a story I had heard at a homeschooling conference. I was speaking to a mother who had accidentally backed over her four-year-old son with her car. The child died later that day, causing indescribable grief to herself, her husband, and their children. And through the tears, I remember how deeply touched I was at the miraculous graces we each are given in such times, when spouses could freely choose to hate. Or to love. To blame. Or to forgive.

It is only through God's great grace that such marriages not only survive, but thrive. I understood how Jay's and my previous crosses helped strengthen our relationship with both Our Lord and each other, and in turn helped us withstand the current cross we bore. Because of our past, I understood that while our entire family was affected by this one incidence, each of us was suffering in our own unique way.

Jay continues to struggle with forgiving himself. He thought the world was angry with him for his mistake. Every time a stranger asks us what happened to Fulton, our first response has always been, "He was burned in a gas can explosion near our burning barrel," and we would leave it at that. Sometimes a few people will press on, at which point we present the story as a public service announcement, such as, "We learned the hard way that it is not safe to use gasoline on a fire, and unfortunately Fulton was a victim of a very poor decision." I try my best to encourage people to ask questions, since it helps normalize Fulton's social interactions with other people, but I also protect my husband out of respect for his suffering.

As you carry your personal cross, are there those around you who cause you to stumble? Is there someone who caused your cross to come about? Are they, perhaps, carrying a related cross you hadn't considered? Have you forgiven them for their role in your suffering? Have you relinquished pride and forgiven yourself for any role you played in bringing the cross upon yourself?

Suffering brings with it raw emotion, exhaustion, and vulnerability, making you easy prey to the darker forces. Suffering rouses pride, pride gives rise to anger, and once you have surrendered to this trap you risk leading yourself and those around you to a battle you cannot win. It is my hope that whatever sufferings you will endure in life, you are able to embrace God's will in all your suffering and allow forgiveness to fully enter your heart. With forgiveness comes healing, and with healing comes peace. Spiritual attacks cannot penetrate a fortress of peace.

I thank You, Lord, for teaching me to quickly recognize the spiritual attacks that come my way. Thank You for keeping me focused on the bigger picture without getting distracted by pointless anger and pride. Your perfect illustration of love and forgiveness on the Cross has taught me that I should not love any less or hold back forgiveness from another, as this would indeed have crippled my journey, and made each of my children's and my husband's cross heavier for them to bear. Thank You for sparing Jay and protecting him in the blast, for sparing Fulton's life and for continuing to trust us with Fulton's soul. Though this suffering is difficult to endure, I pray we bring You glory through it.

***

Saint Michael the Archangel, defend us in battle. Be our safeguard against the wickedness and snares of the devil. May God rebuke him, we humbly pray. And do thou, O Prince of the Heavenly Hosts, cast into Hell Satan and all the evil spirits who prowl through the world seeking the ruin of souls.
Amen.

CHAPTER 19

"What we need is a cup of understanding, a barrel
of love, and an ocean of patience."
—*St. Francis de Sales*

The dried Bermuda grass shivered in the January wind; the frost turned its golden, lifeless blades to silver before the wintery sun slowly melted its steely sheen away. As the winds blew, the blades sorrowfully bowed to the patches of ashen black where their fellow blades once grew. But no one, not even those blades of grass, acknowledged what else lay on the ground that first week.

The remnants of a tiny striped t-shirt, most of its cotton fibers long gone, abandoned to fend for itself in the cold. Shapeless masses of burnt flesh still clung to what was left of the garment, speaking of the violence in which it was frantically torn from a little boy's body as he burned. Alone.

Those who were left in Oklahoma to cope with the aftermath of that tragic day avoided the remains of Fulton's clothing. What it may have meant to each family member probably varied greatly—from repulsion to denial—and so it remained for almost a week while my family worked through their initial shock over what had happened.

I learned, one year later, what my children did that day after Fulton and I left in the ambulance. CJ helped the first responders put the grassfire out. Shannon whisked Marialina out of the kitchen before she saw too much or got in the way. Virginia made herself useful, getting the clean sheet, packing my purse and starting a prayer chain. My mother had to drive Jay to a local hospital in Arkansas, leaving my five to fend for themselves.

"The house reeked of gasoline," my oldest daughter told me. "And Marialina started throwing up." Mari was too young to understand what had actually happened, but the fumes were strong enough to make her sick. Virginia took care of her while the others sat in the living room or in their bedrooms in silence.

"They should have gone over to my house, away from the fumes!" my mother exclaimed. She lived in her own home, which was attached to our house by a breezeway. "I had no idea!"

"I felt like I never knew what was going on," another child protested, while another child privately suffered nightmares and symptoms of post-traumatic stress for an entire year before finally coming to me for help.

And so it went. Little pieces of that time period came together, offered by each family member, which slowly revealed to me a startling reality I had never before considered.

How did my other family members cope with the trauma? I tried to help as best I could, but each of their sufferings were different, and it was difficult to identify ways I could help from over six hundred miles away. Several months after returning home, I realized the vast differences in the ways each family member actually suffered. This new awareness opened my eyes to how I could have been a better mother to them all, and a better wife to my husband. I pray they forgive me for my shortfalls.

Jay, my six children, and I were all formed uniquely by God Himself. Each of us was created with our personal vices and virtues, strengths and weaknesses. We were growing spiritually, but at different rates. We were being refined, but by different, private fires known only to ourselves and to Our Lord.

One accident. Eight crosses. It was a humbling moment to realize how much we all had to be healed. I am still becoming aware of bits and pieces of the cross each child bore that first year after the accident, and continue to carry to this day.

I would like to say we all made it through with flying colors, but that would not be the truth. Resentment, post-traumatic stress, falling behind in school—these were a few of the added burdens some of us carried at that time. There are many things I would have done differently, knowing what I know now. But we did the best we could, and there was always an abundance of love and prayer, which covered a multitude of our faults. Deo gratias.

I realized that just as Jesus suffered His agony in the garden alone, so must we all suffer. Even if our crosses are family tragedies, each family member ultimately suffers by themselves. We are each created as unique beings and therefore operate on different levels spiritually. Levels of faith, hope, and charity vary greatly, as does our ability to endure physical and emotional pain. Where one may be weak, another may be strong. Keep this fact ever before you as you suffer, as this will help you understand your loved ones.

While my family was learning to cope with the aftermath of the accident in their own ways, I had learned that even the families within the burn hospital suffered in a multitude of ways. Yes, we shared the same hospital floor. Every one of us had children who suffered similar injuries. We all were away from home, had worries of infection, feared for our children's survival and had financial stresses. Yet we were also very alone.

There was another patient two rooms down whose daughter was admitted the same day as Fulton. This family was from Mexico, but unlike most of the families from there, the father's English was clear and concise. Their home caught fire, the child's grandmother died, and his daughter was immediately flown to Texas.

One day we were comparing notes and experiences, trying to give each other hope in dismal circumstances. I was lamenting the fact that they were unable to get Fulton to breathe on his own, and that his ears could not be saved. Tearfully he shared that his daughter was having her fingers amputated that day, on both of her hands. "She is my only child. My princess. At least your son is still intact." *Yes—yes he is, praise God!* The breathing will eventually resolve itself, I was sure, but once you lose your fingers, you have a whole new set of issues to overcome.

But his heartbreak continued. "Her stomach, everywhere," he motioned all around his back and waist with his hands, "all burned so badly." He closed his eyes, now glistening, and his pain restricted his voice to almost a whisper. "Once the scars are set, she will not be able to have children."

There were trails of tears down our cheeks. The pain we were experiencing for our children was similar, yet worlds apart. Fulton, Lord willing, will be able to sprout new branches onto our family tree. But, unless a tremendous miracle should occur, this man's family tree would grow no more.

It was a good reminder that we were all grieving over our children in some way. For him, he grieved the loss of her hands and the end of his family line. His dreams of grandchildren and leaving his legacy behind to future generations literally went up in flames before him. For me, it was the loss of Fulton's face, his ears, and a portion of his childhood. But while I mourned these losses, I was emboldened by the example of the other children who were far more advanced in the healing process. The loss that I felt every day was being replaced with grace and hope beyond what I ever could have imagined.

I learned early on to try not to impose my way of coping upon others. The temptation is strong to want to ease the suffering of those we care about, but what works for us may not be what works for others. Allow loved ones the time they need to grieve in the manner of their choosing, and keep the lines of communication open. Watch each other for signs of despair and intervene if one seems to be headed down a dangerous path. But otherwise, choose to simply love those around you for who they are and respect the time they spend in their own Garden of Gethsemane.

Each of us will suffer in life. As you experience your own Passion, remember always that those around you are suffering as well. Be prepared for the temptations to lash out at others or accuse others of not understanding your pain. It may very well be that they do not understand, but it is not their fault. They are struggling in ways you may not understand. Simply focus on the love that keeps them nearby. All else can be forgiven.

***

Lord, make me an instrument of Thy peace;
Where there is hatred, let me sow love;
Where there is injury, pardon;
Where there is error, the truth;
Where there is doubt, the faith;
Where there is despair, hope;
Where there is darkness, light;
And where there is sadness, joy.

O Divine Master,
Grant that I may not so much seek
To be consoled, as to console;
To be understood, as to understand;
To be loved as to love.

For it is in giving that we receive;
It is in pardoning that we are pardoned;
And it is in dying that we are born to eternal life. Amen.

CHAPTER 20

"Sometimes God's love looks very ugly on the surface."
—Cassandra Poppe

The necessity for suffering has been a topic Catholic Saints and sinners alike have pondered ever since that fateful day on Calvary. It is all in God's hands—His divine plan. But suffering is not a plan most people understand on the surface. "Where was God?" is the common cry when disaster strikes. And this cry continues to go unanswered until the instinct to look only at one's own pain finally turns and looks at pain through God's heart. Once this shift takes place, this suffering is transformed into a divine love that one is able to accept, and sometimes able to even embrace with anticipation. What is it God is calling me to do? Am I worthy of this calling?

I recently gave a talk at a charity event on ways to grow in holiness. A large portion of this talk, of course, was focused on accepting God's will in all things that come our way. This is by no means an easy thing to do, and the only thing that makes it possible is to change your way of seeing what lies before you.

For most of us, our crosses come in fits and starts, with minor pains and worries in between. And there is much grace to be gained when you treat these crosses as a training ground for larger crosses that may come to you in your future.

But what happens when that larger cross comes to you? When, through your own fault or an accident, God allows suffering to come? When it feels as though God looks at your life and says, "No."

"No" to your life as you are living it.

And "no" to your dreams of the future.

These crosses are not subtle. A child becomes gravely ill. A spouse is in a devastating car accident. You have been diagnosed with cancer.

For our family, that explosive "No" came through that little gas can, and our lives forever changed. I was separated from my family by over 600 miles for three months, sons and daughters struggling to finish school on their own, a little boy clinging to life, and me, desperately clinging to the foot of the Cross.

Where else could I run but to the foot of the Cross—that source of perfect consolation? Where what it means to love and achieve perfect unity of God's became so clear? It is no surprise so few remained at Our Lord's feet on Good Friday. "Thy will be done" is a bitter pill to swallow when perfect unity is not yet achieved.

However, as we strive for this perfect unity, we learn what this surrender looks like, and the bitterness becomes sweet. We must remind ourselves that it is precisely in the times we are tried by fire that we grow in holiness and become Godly people. These times can be very difficult. But be not afraid! Our Lord has given us a coping mechanism—a filter of sorts—to help us through those tough times. This filter is love! Take God's love for you, make that love your filter, and train yourself to see the loving hand of God in everything that happens to you.

Unfortunately we often have too many other filters preventing us from finding that love. Filters of fear, a desire for comfort, and especially pride. When we see life's sufferings through these filters, our pain is multiplied and we are not at peace simply because these filters force us to focus on ourselves instead of God.

St. Frances de Sales had a deep understanding of the intensity in which Almighty God loves us and how He wants us to embrace the crosses that come our way. In fact, the Saint even goes so far as to describe suffering as an alms of the all-merciful love of God.

Suffering as an alms of the all-merciful love of God. What a powerful concept! When I hear the word 'alms', an image of Sweet William comes to my mind. Sweet William was a homeless man I walked past twice a day, every day, when I worked at my corporate job in Chicago. Not only burdened with his homeless plight, he also suffered from kidney disease and was completely blind. I power-walked almost two miles between the train station and my office, passing hundreds of others bustling to and from their high paying financial jobs, and none were more joyful than he. Rain or shine, he constantly sung the praises of Almighty God, thankful for whatever alms rattled in his can. And thankful when it was empty.

Sweet William understood that his lot was that of the life of Job. He knew that he could turn all trials that happened to him into a balm to a soul being perfected. And just as the money, meals, and changes of clothes were alms from me to help him in his temporal need, his blindness, disease, homelessness, and hunger were the spiritual alms, allowed by Our Lord, to ultimately help his soul. And what a beautiful soul God perfected in him!

Truly, our souls are like beggars on the street. Diseased and blinded with sin, starving for union with Our Lord, and longing for the protective shelter only Heaven can offer, we go through life seeking alms from Our King. He drops graces and consolations into our cans to strengthen us, and we rejoice over these blessings. But we must also rejoice when the sufferings and trials He allows are dropped in our cans, for all of His alms, whatever form they may come in, are for our ultimate good.

"Every tribulation whichever comes our way either is sent to be medicinal, if we will take it as such, or may become medicinal, if we will make it such, or is better than medicinal, unless we forsake it," says the wise St. Thomas More

Forearmed with this knowledge, whenever people asked me "How can God allow such suffering?" when talking about Fulton, I could honestly respond by saying, "Sometimes God's love looks very ugly on the surface."

Remembering those first few days in the hospital, I can assure you there is nothing physically beautiful about a child missing more than ninety percent of the skin on his little face. Yet the graces, strength and consolations that came with that cross proved to me how dearly He loves us and that He truly desired that our hearts be refined through this trial. Not as a punishment—but because He loved us enough to draw us closer to Him in ways He never could, had the suffering never come.

Once the pain subsided, we began to see what Our Lord was calling us to do. He does not call us to simply suffer. Instead, He uses that pain to help us grow and glorify Him through our suffering. Our need to lean on Him draws us closer, and as we heave our cross, He aids us, and in that aid we feel His love, and become ever-closer to him. We learn how to offer our pain, our cross to Him, as Jesus did for us. And by being united in God's will, through this submission to Him, He gives the graces to get through our tragedy and arrive where he ultimately wants us—at His side.

For some, the idea of offering up our suffering will be understood and embraced immediately. For others, it may take years. Others may never understand it, which is OK because in the end, God does not owe us explanations. But do not give up. Do not doubt His wisdom. And never doubt His love. It is there, waiting for you always. And once you find this love, you cannot help but find ways to return this love to Him.

Much of our time in Galveston occurred during Lent, and the significance was not lost on me. There were times when I truly felt alone in my suffering. And as the weeks progressed and Fulton became more aware of his own suffering and limitations, I am sure he felt alone as well. We were inseparable, and yet worlds apart. Being a small child, Fulton could not have been expected to ease my pain. I was his parent, and it was my job to ease his suffering in any way I could.

Once Fulton and I left the ICU, we were required to live within a few blocks of the hospital to have continued, instant access to every aspect of care he still needed. Jay was 600 miles away and I had no shoulder to cry on during these difficult weeks, no one to share the daily burdens of the painful hours-long bandaging procedures, or the constant administration of multiple medications. The utter lack of sleep was exhausting, and it took every ounce of my waning strength to crawl out of bed at 4:30 each morning, steeling myself for the day's activities.

And what of Fulton? Too young to understand the higher levels of suffering, all he knew was misery. Nauseous, but forced to swallow countless medications throughout the day. Never hungry yet constantly pestered to eat. Open wounds that did not heal meant torturous bandage changes and scrubbing twice a day. Exhaustion hit him as well, as he averaged only about four hours of sleep a night. Physical therapy, making him move against the scars that insisted on healing in incorrect ways. Pressure garments that were tight, itchy, and uncomfortable. Painful scar massages and mouth stretchers. He was often crabby when we were alone, but at least he was more cheerful when interacting with the hospital personnel.

Since it was just the two of us, all I could do was try to be as positive as possible. Sometimes, when the bandages were clinging to his wounds and it would take forty minutes just to get them all removed, my prayers took on a selfish tone. *Where, Lord, is Thy consolation?* I tried thinking of other things while I cared for Fulton. Flower gardens, swimming with dolphins, a walk on the beach. But this kind of disconnect, by wishing I were somewhere else, ultimately caused me to grow weary with his care. I was crabby and frustrated, and Fulton could tell.

I soon realized that there was not temporal consolation to be found. Only love. Love for my son. Love for Our Lady. And Love for our Lord in His Passion. And I prayed that my acts of love in caring for Fulton would be a consolation to Our Lord as He carried His Cross.

I recalled those days so many years before when I attempted to care for my family by selfless service while we were struggling in Arkansas, and the pure joy I felt when tending to my daily duties as though I were doing them for Our Lord. So I began caring for Fulton in the same manner, using my imagination to also tend to Our Lord. And in doing so, these daily burdens became almost beautiful. Hope returned! I took on the heart of Our Blessed Mother, washing the wounds of her Son, offering up the heartbreak I felt and placing it at Our Lord's crucified feet. Responding to Fulton's screams with soothing tones, trying not to get frustrated as he constantly pushed me away, it was the only way I could survive each day, knowing all was ultimately being done for the love of God. As I bathed Fulton's wounds, I also bathed the sacred wounds of Our Lord, praying I could give Him some level of consolation as I tended to my son. This was how I survived. It was not perfect, though, as I had my moments of weeping and even arguing with Fulton, but keeping Our Lord's Cross and His love ever before me truly helped me persevere.

Those weeks were filled with moments of mortification, and I had to remind myself, sometimes several times a day, that each moment of suffering was simply another alms in my can. A chance to die to self. A cure for self-love. And each moment was a chance to choose to stay at His feet to give to Him another portion of my heart in gratitude for the love He has already shown me.

My will and my love are still not completely His to claim. It is a daily tug of war within me to continue on this journey. But through all we have experienced, I rejoice in the fact that I am able to offer up my suffering to the One who loves me most and wants nothing more than for me to spend eternity in perfect joy with Him in Heaven. Blessed be God, forever!

***

Dear Lord, St. Claude de la Colombiere once said, "It is only God who can sanctify us, and it is no small thing to desire sincerely that He may do all that is necessary for this, for of ourselves we have neither sufficient light nor sufficient strength." How true this is! You created me to be with You in Heaven forever. And being my Creator, only You know all that I must endure to bring me Home. When I cannot see suffering through Your love for me, place upon my heart the Crucified Lord, that I may ever be reminded of Your great love. Make me desire to suffer for You and give me the strength to endure this trial of sanctification. For without Your love and Your help, I am lost. Amen.

CHAPTER 21

"Miracles are a retelling in small letters of the very same story which is written across the whole world in letters too large for some of us to see."
—C.S. Lewis

<u>*Care Page Entry Posted Jan 18, 2013*</u>

"Please keep your prayers coming—we are seeing the most amazing healing taking place already! His lips and eyelids look (dare I say it) beautiful! Even the nurse was amazed at his right eyelid this morning, as it seems to be regenerating itself. I was grinning ear to ear today. God is so good! (Venerable Fulton Sheen, please beg the Lord to heal my baby!)

It will be a long and painful journey but my faith grows stronger with each day that passes, and I am confident that as long as I remain firmly planted at the foot of His Cross, His will shall be done through me.

Lord, forgive my occasional selfish pleas if they are not in accordance with Your will. It is Your will that I embrace this Cross, and so I accept it. Just give me the grace to persevere."

There were, indeed, many selfish prayers. Many times the nurses would find me on the floor, stroking his one good foot and crying as I prayed, "Venerable Fulton Sheen, please heal my baby!" Inspired by the Engstrom family's story about their miraculous healing that took place through Venerable Fulton Sheen's intercession, I had complete faith that if it were to be God's will, a miracle would be granted to us as well.

I kept this good man's second class relic in Fulton's room, and prayed for a miracle to be worked through his intercession. I had immersed myself in the writings and stories of the Saints for years, and I knew what Our Lord was capable of doing. I hoped beyond hope for something big—complete, miraculous regeneration of his skin. I could almost see us walking out of the hospital, completely healed and praising God the whole way. It would be glorious!

Please, Lord, send us an astounding miracle to help convert hearts! What better way to show others Your power and mercy than to give this beautiful little boy fresh skin, defying all medical reasoning!

OK Lord, complete healing may not be Your will. So, maybe You could just give him back his ears?

Maybe?

Thy will be done, Lord. Sustain me.

He opened an eye again today—that is enough.

And I am grateful.

I never lost hope in a miracle, but sometimes the pressure became too much. "Keep praying," people would say. "I just know God will work a miracle through your little boy!" But weeks came and went with no discernable miracles taking place. The very fact that I did not lose my mind was enough of a miracle for me, but Fulton's growing cheering squad was getting restless. *Why, Lord, are miracles for others and not for us?* It wasn't a toddler-tantrum sort of question. It was not even voiced in a sorrowful tone. I was simply seeking His will and for clarification as to why He chose not to heal my son in the way He has chosen to heal so many others throughout our rich Church history. What did it mean?

I would find myself frequently pondering the mysteries of God's ways and wondered how His will would be played out. Would Fulton's story be like St. Kateri who lived her entire life with scars? Or would his story be of the boy whose skin was miraculously healed through St. Kateri's intercession?

Would He work through St. Frances Cabrini again as He did for the infant Peter Smith whose eyes were chemically burned? That baby's sight and skin were restored to their original infant beauty, scar free. Could she obtain for us such a blessed favor from God?

Would Venerable Fulton Sheen obtain a visible miracle from God as he did for the Engstrom family? Or will the greater miracle of conversion occur where only Our Lord can see. There were so many friends in Heaven to ask for help, so many miracles to dream about, so many possibilities!

I was firmly set in my swing, still wanting a physical miracle, but also praying *Thy will be done*, ready to accept that sometimes we have to take the long road to joy. Either way, I knew it would be an amazing ride. I just had to be patient and see if He wanted to make known His presence in some tangible way.

One direct intervention indeed came, but I was riding that swing so high, the breezes caused by my perpetual movements between high hopes and resignation swirled around me in such a way that it made it almost impossible for me to detect the gentle breath of God as He quietly did His work.

The first few days after being discharged from the ICU were probably the hardest days of all. I had to admit my weakness and accept the fact that I was a miserable mother. Up until they handed him over to me each day, I was the good mother. The fun mother. The one who tried to make his day a little brighter. But at the Ronald McDonald House, everything changed. I was suddenly the medicine mother. The scrubbing and bandaging mother. The mean mother.

All he would do each day was sit in his little umbrella stroller and stare. He would doze off from time to time, but he had to be sitting upright as much as possible to help him regain the torso muscle strength he had lost. I also had to give him medications every hour, and he had to be sitting up for those. He was silent. No matter how much I chatted with him, all he would do was sit and stare at the floor. Or at me.

It was a tiny hotel-like room and filling up quickly with all of his medical supplies. I could hardly get around his stroller without stumbling. The lighting was dim and depressing, and there was nothing for him to do but watch movies on my computer. But he was not even interested in that.

At least in the hospital he had started to talk to me more, and we actually had many cheerful days together. But now it was a nightmare. Every tick of the clock was one tick closer to a new torture to begin and I could imagine what was going on in his little mind. *Would this hour mean a feeding? Or medication? Please, please, don't make it a bandage change.*

There was a sink in our room, and every time I turned the water on, he would wiggle a little, beginning his protest. The nonstick bandages were still sticking like they had been superglued to his head and I had to begin the painful process of placing soaking washcloths onto his head to start softening the bandages. It never worked very well, but what were my choices?

The carpeting was always damp, his shirt and stroller were dripping and we were both in tears. It was a two-hour process of soaking and pulling off each piece of gauze, and then soaping and rinsing his head and other wound sites that had not healed yet, all while sitting in his stroller. He moved from a scream to a whimper and back. Agony. And because he was so loud, moving him to the bathroom was not an option. Other people had to use the bathroom too, and the tiled walls made his cries echo throughout the entire floor. There was nowhere else to go.

Bandage changing time was the only time he said anything to me at all. "I don't love you," he would say. And my heart would break. I knew on one level he was just responding to the fact that I was the one causing him the pain, and I understood that. But I also understood that at those moments, he actually meant what he said. I was, truly, the meanest mother in the world to him.

Praise God, I had given him over to Our Lady—his mother who was never mean, who never caused him pain, who persevered at his side, even when I felt I could not. And truly, Our Lady was watching over him in a special way one cold February morning, minding the things that truly mattered while I fretted about the more temporal issues of the day. And it was Our Lady through whom Our Lord gave us that gentle miracle.

It was surgery day once again. The morning began like all others—dark, cold, miserable. Also, unmercifully early. We moved slowly and quietly, although many other tenants at the Ronald McDonald House were also beginning their day. I took his blood pressure and gave him his heart medication, but nothing else. "No more medicine for you today, Buddy!" I cheerfully announced. He slept in his button up shirt again, since there were no button up pajamas available in the stores. I did not even bother changing his clothes. It was just too much work with all the bandages. The morning would be stressful enough.

An expert at playing the waiting room game, I gathered what I thought I would need: book, notebook, pen, cell phone, wallet.

And holy water.

What? Of course. Bless him with holy water. Good idea.

He slumped in his stroller behind me while I brushed my teeth. I had to remember to pack his blood pressure charts and a change of clean clothes. *And holy water. Lourdes water. Yes, that too.*

I then packed his bandage bag. Shriners supplied me with everything I needed to care for his wounds, but I had to carry these supplies with me wherever I went. Ointments, nonstick pads, Q-Tips, scissors, rolls of gauze and fresh Ace bandages. *Lourdes water. Before you forget.*

I sighed, feeling somewhat annoyed at the intrusion. I just knew I was going to forget something if I kept getting distracted. A few people blessed us with bottles of holy water right after the accident and I used it from time to time, although admittedly not as often as I probably should have. I quickly dug through my drawer and pulled out one of the tiny bottles I had, half filled, and dropped it in my medical bag.

No. Lourdes water.

I paused a moment. I then recalled my experience when the word 'prepare' kept coming to me and felt I should listen once again to this inner urging placed upon my heart. And so I obeyed. I went to my other drawer where I kept all my sacramentals and found the glass bottle with Our Lady of Lourdes water in it. I gently blessed him, careful not to wake him up.

I tucked his blankets tightly around him and wheeled him to the elevator. *Lord, please protect my boy today. Please guide the hands of the surgeons. And please prevent him from throwing up.*

The hospital's security guard was waiting for us outside the Ronald McDonald House. I lifted Fulton carefully out of his stroller, buckled him securely into the car seat, and we headed the four blocks to the hospital.

Everything proceeded as usual in the beginning. Just a quick surgery, two hours tops, they said. And they would send us back to the Ronald McDonald House when he recovered. No problem.

They were wrong.

His surgery wound up lasting well over six hours, and no one came to explain why he had not returned. By this time, though, I was used to changes in the plans and took it all in stride. I concluded that things were going well and they were on a roll, or they found something that needed attention that they did not previously plan on addressing. Whatever was happening, I was at peace.

Finally, a doctor approached. "His surgery went well overall," he explained, "but we will be readmitting him to the burn unit for a few nights. We discovered his blood has reached a highly toxic level of potassium and we want to keep an eye on him. It is actually a good thing he had his surgery scheduled today, or we may not have caught it."

Again, what would have sent me into a tailspin of worry before, only caused me to raise an eyebrow now. Relieved they caught the blood issue early, I was resigned to just wait and see. Had I known how serious his condition was, I probably would have worried more, but ignorance maintained my peace.

I was actually relieved he was admitted, as I did not have to be terrified of his new skin grafts. They did a lot of work on the left side of his head, patchwork on his face, and a three-inch square on the back of his neck. My prayers were focused on no infection and that these last wound sites would finally heal. Once his wounds were closed and secure, I hoped I would feel more capable of taking care of him myself. But trying to function at a hypervigilant level was exhausting.

The next few hours after surgery were spent at his side, choosing which movies to watch and distracting him from the fact he was back in the hospital. He was agitated and tearful when I had to leave him that night, but once again the nursing night staff was able to put us both at ease.

Relieved he was back in the capable hands of the nurses, I collapsed into bed that night and slept soundly.

A few weeks later, we were at our daily tubroom visit and the head surgeon mentioned this particular surgery and Fulton's hyperkalemia. "Ah! That was the day Fulton stopped breathing on the operating table," he casually mentioned to one of the other surgeons. Everyone straightened up and solemnly nodded as they remembered that day. *What are they talking about?* I thought. *No one told me this!* The doctors continued their huddle, leaving me to wonder what I was supposed to do with this new piece of information.

As several weeks passed, my mind would occasionally return to the surgeon's comment. I finally decided to put the pieces together and sought out the entry I had written for that particular day. I was stunned to realize a miracle of sorts was revealed to me. Our Lady of Lourdes, in her most humble manner, asked me to put my trust in her, and she rewarded me for my blind faith. Not only was that a surgery day, but it was also February 11, the Feast of Our Lady of Lourdes!

I ended my CarePages post in this way:

> *"It is so humbling to see how little miracles are so easily missed. I prayed so hard for big miracles of astounding healing, I didn't see the gift that was hidden, yet so much bigger than just some fixed skin. He lives and I am grateful.*
>
> *God be praised, he didn't die. Thank you, Our Lady of Lourdes! (OK, I'll stop crying now)*
>
> *God is good—always!"*

Fulton had been suffering from hyperkalemia. This can occur in burn patients, due to the massive tissue destruction that takes place at the time of injury. When cells are destroyed, they release potassium into the body, and if the kidneys are not functioning properly, this excess potassium can build up in the bloodstream, causing chemical and electrical imbalances throughout the body. The only way to test for this imbalance is through blood tests, which, had he not gone into surgery that day, he would not have had.

Fulton had been silently but steadily deteriorating since his release. Since we returned to the hospital every day and he was seen by several doctors who did not seem overly concerned about his developing symptoms, I assumed it was either a normal stage for him to go through or a matter of poor health management on my part. I also considered it was all simply due to him suffering from utter exhaustion, which was certainly understandable. I had no idea something far more serious was building up in my son's body.

But Our Lady did.

If he hadn't had surgery that day, if he had crashed while alone with me, what would I have done? Would I have been able to administer CPR on his already wounded body and mouth until medics arrived? Or would I have awoken that morning to find my son lifeless in his crib?

Was this an actual miracle in the literal sense? No. But it was without a doubt a moment in time where God had chosen to gently ask for me to cooperate in His greater plan, to help myself and others see how intricately entwined the spiritual and temporal could be, and how much He esteems Our Lady's intercessions. Whether Our Lady was warning me that his potassium levels were getting out of control or she foresaw something happening on the operating table that day, I do not know. But I am eternally grateful for her intercession that day, for the promptings she gave to me, and her healing touch.

There were many other beautiful lights along our path, and I pray your path will be well lit too. Remain ever-mindful of the still, small voice within and heed its promptings when it urges you to pray, and make special use of a sacramental or a Sacrament when you feel called to do so. You are never closer to Our Lord than when you willingly embrace your cross, and His graces will pour over you when you make frequent use of such helps.

***

Our Lady of Lourdes, your miraculous waters have healed countless souls, bringing them to the faith, and many suffering bodies have been healed through your intercession as well. I thank you for the careful watch you have placed over Fulton and I am comforted knowing he is cherished by such a loving Mother. I place Fulton and all my children under the safety of your mantle, and pray you take them as your own children, that they one day be safely brought into your loving arms. Amen.

Chapter 22

"Misfortune is never mournful to the soul that accepts it; for such do always see that in every cloud is an angel's face."
—*St. Jerome*

One day, several weeks after returning home, my mother, Fulton, and I stopped into Burger King for a quick lunch. They had an indoor playground and of course he wanted to play. His head wounds were still open, and I kept it wrapped in bandages and gauze, and he wore a wide brimmed hat to help keep the bandages in place and clean, and to protect his skin from the sun. He disappeared into the maze of tubes, and I tried to focus on my lunch, but my ears strained to catch portions of the conversations taking place beyond my eyesight.

I caught a few of the words exchanged between Fulton and an older boy. And then I heard Fulton say, "Give me back my hat." My stomach sank. Some scuffling and muttering, and then again, "I need my hat. Give it back!"

Nausea hit me as I walked to the foot of the slide. "Please give him his hat back," I called up the tube. Fulton made a distraught sound, as if he were about to cry. "Give him his hat. Now!" I said it loud enough so the child's mother and friend would hear me. But they were no help. Finally the child zipped down the slide and headed around to the other side of the playroom, carefully avoiding my Mama Bear stare. Then slowly, cautiously, Fulton scooted down, hat in hand and tears in his eyes.

"Are you done playing, honey?" I asked as I helped him with his hat.

"I want to go home," he whispered. We quickly left the restaurant and as I buckled him into his seat, he asked, "Why was that boy mean to me?"

"I think maybe he did not understand what happened to you. And maybe he is not a very happy child and he thinks that being mean will make him feel better. Do you want to pray for him? And maybe to his Guardian Angel to help him?"

He nodded, and we prayed together as we headed home. I tried to keep the conversation light to distract him, but inside my heart was breaking. He had been through so much, and this was the first time he had ever been bullied in his life. I wanted to curl up with him in my arms and protect him forever. But I knew I could not do that. We simply needed a better plan.

Shriner's Hospital had been a haven for Fulton as he healed. Every possible need was taken care of, and he had quickly accepted the hospital and our rental house as his new home. Everyone around him was either burned or caring for the patients, which made him feel like he was an important member of a large community. No one stared or made comments about his scars. He was simply accepted for who he was.

When we came home, however, he was rather surprised at how the real world reacted to his appearance. Before he was burned, a trip to the grocery store was rather mundane and uneventful. Now, however, it had become a game of trying to avoid stares and comments from strangers in the store. Only the game was not very fun.

"Aah! Daddy! Why is he so ugly?" and, "Look, Mommy! A monkey!" are just two examples of actual comments we have heard. That, coupled with the constant staring of young children and a few adults made him very self-conscious. I soon realized that trying to help Fulton cope emotionally with all the changes in his life was going to be another cross we would have to bear. I could not accurately determine just how much these unfortunate encounters effected his gentle soul, and I was at a loss as to how to help him. Praise God, he has yet to show any signs of long-term Post Traumatic Stress, but the constant attention he seemed to attract began to wear him down.

We had practiced simple answers to people's questions before we left the hospital. "I was burned, but I am getting better," was short and to the point, and he was comfortable using that answer to most people's questions. But Jay and I realized that even though he was good at reciting his quick explanation, he really did not have anywhere to go with it. Sometimes people would ask more questions or simply walk away, but it soon became apparent that something else was needed.

He needed something to help him come away from such encounters feeling better about himself rather than spouting trained answers to satisfy others' curiosity. A recurring comment Fulton would say was, "They don't know who I am or what happened to me."

Then one day, an idea came to me. "Fulton, do you want to tell people about yourself and about the accident?" We talked about what he wanted to say and I wrote it all down. "How about I give you a card with your story on it so you can give it to the people who ask you questions?" He was not quite sure what I had in mind but readily agreed. I read to him the story he wanted to tell people, and then asked, "What else do you want to tell them?"

"How to be safe with fire!" he quickly responded.

I hadn't thought of that, but I instantly saw the value in what he said. Not only were we going to give people a little piece of Fulton's story, but we would also provide them with some valuable information as well. The people he would meet would come away with more than they had expected, and Fulton would feel as if he was helping others stay safe, thus giving him more control of the encounters and giving him a sense of purpose.

I studied up on various burn facts and learned that 75% of burns were due to scalding. We remembered several patients at Shriners who were scalded and decided that sharing some information about scalding might help the most number of people. On the back of the cards, I also included some basic first aid tips to help people who were seriously burned. Next, I included before and after photos of Fulton to help other children see that he looked very much like them before the accident and was the same person he always was, only now he had scars. Then off to the printers I went.

The day we received his cards was a pivotal moment in Fulton's emotional healing. He finally had a tool, his 'burn cards' as he calls them, to help him find his place in this world.

I will never forget the first time he handed one of his cards out to another child. In the car as we headed to the mall, we practiced different ways he could present the card to people. I gave him a few ideas but really wanted him to find the words with which he would be most comfortable. As we headed into the mall, I said, "OK buddy. This is it. Who are you going to help today?"

We made it through several stores and received many stares and smiles, but no real opportunity presented itself to Fulton. Finally, we were standing in line at The Children's Place, waiting to make a purchase, when a mother and her four-year-old daughter got in line behind us. The little girl could not take her eyes off of Fulton, and I could tell the mother was conflicted. Should she tell her daughter to stop staring, thus making Fulton uncomfortable? Or let her daughter stare and not say anything at all? Fulton became aware of the situation, stood up a little straighter, looked the little girl right into her eyes and said, "People sometimes wonder what happened to me. I was burned." As he said this, he raised his hand to me and snapped his fingers, gesturing for me to hand him a card. I fumbled in my purse for a moment, handed him the card, and he said, "Here. Take this. This will help you be safe." The little girl took the card silently, and handed it up to her mother who was staring open mouthed at me in surprise.

"Wow!" she said. "Thank you!" She proceeded to show her daughter the card and talk about what was on it, instantly diverting attention from Fulton and onto the information on the card. Fulton squeezed my hand and beamed up at me. "I did it!" he said. I was one proud mama, and relished the look of pure joy on his face.

The mother and child were instantly at ease and the three of them chatted about the information on the card, his burns, and how he can still assemble Lego sets, even while wearing his pressure garments.

As time passed and he grew more practiced at using his burn cards, I began to notice a wonderful side effect his cards were having on people. Before, children who stared or made comments were hushed or even yelled at by their parents. A few times I even witnessed more physical forms of punishment once the family reached the parking lot.

I am a mother of seven and know all too well how a child's unexpected behavior can cause a lot of embarrassment. I felt bad for the parents, of course, but I felt worse for the children, as did Fulton who felt horrible about being the apparent cause of such punishments.

The Good God created children to be naturally curious. When they see something different, they want to know why. And it is the parent's job to teach them what they need to know. But when it comes to dealing with a person with a handicap, or one who looks different, the child's natural curiosity can cause a lot of embarrassment. The unfortunate and unintended result of this embarrassment teaches the children that people with differences are to be ignored ("Stop looking at him!") or should cause them to feel uncomfortable or should be avoided for some reason.

Surprisingly, Fulton's burn cards took care of this problem as well. As soon as a parent has a burn card in hand, the parent regains control of the situation and of their own child. They are able to direct the conversation towards either Fulton's story to discuss how he is very much like other children, or to the safety facts. The parents and children instantly become more relaxed and everyone leaves the encounter with smiles. The incredible success of these cards made us realize that perhaps we were to help other children as well, and we have since created Friendly Face Forward—a small company providing social integration cards to whomever needs them, free of charge.

Now that Fulton has grown more comfortable in his new skin, he has used his burn cards to start longer conversations, which, on occasion, have lasted twenty minutes or more. There is something very powerful about visible suffering. Fulton's presence gives hope to those around him. He wears his suffering on his face and body just as Christ bore His wounds on the Cross for all to see. I am always amazed at the stories he draws out of people at such a young age. I firmly believe it is in these conversations that Our Lord's will is revealed.

One afternoon, my mother took Fulton out for ice cream. There was an older couple in the restaurant when Fulton walked in, and they immediately took notice, said hello, and offered to buy him ice cream. A conversation started and the man revealed that he too was burned several years ago in a gasoline explosion at a gas station. His torso was severely burned and he had a scar on his neck and cheek, of which he was very self-conscious. He was struggling, still healing from his pain, but trying to let Fulton know he was not alone.

Fulton then handed him a burn card and they chatted some more. By this time, the man was in tears. He clutched the card and vowed to keep it forever and would look at it whenever he felt sad.

Fulton's steadfast faith, despite his suffering, is a powerful source of evangelization to those who come in contact with him. Without realizing it, he invites many hearts to look at life's trials in a different light, considering how intimately God is involved in both our pains and our triumphs.

I pray this childlike faith remains with him always.

Fulton's natural acceptance of what has happened, coupled with his innocence, continues to offer hope to those around him. No one escapes life without having something to suffer, and God is using Fulton to show other suffering souls that their crosses can be carried with dignity and even joy. And this, I believe, is part of God's greater plan.

***

Lord, there are days when I am overwhelmed to think of what You might wish for me to nurture in my son. May he grow in purpose, gathering strength in his little victories each day. Continue to groom him for Your greater plan, and help him evangelize Your love to all those with whom he comes into contact. I thank You, Lord, for allowing Fulton's angelic face to brighten my mornings and pray that he grows to realize Your holy will in his life, that he may one day smile with You in Heaven. Amen.

CHAPTER 23

"Teach us, Good Lord, to give and not count the cost;
to fight and not to heed the wounds; to toil and not to
seek for rest; to labor and not to ask for any reward
save that of knowing that we do thy will."
—*St Ignatius of Loyola*

While Catholics in general may not embrace suffering, the Catholic faith itself teaches us of the immense value in suffering. We have crucifixes to remind us of Our Lord's suffering and sacrifice, inspiring us to mortify ourselves for love of Him. We understand that suffering is a part of life and a tool we must use well for the sanctification of our soul. Others avoid suffering, seeing it as either a punishment or from Satan. But whatever the true cause, we must always remember that all suffering is allowed by Our Lord. And if He allows it to happen, we must treat it as an invaluable opportunity to grow in holiness and give glory to God. No matter what.

I do not say this lightly, as it is indeed both a joy and a burden to be trusted by Our Lord. He requires much of those He loves—sometimes more than we think we can handle. But we may rest in the fact that as long as we remain firmly at His side, all things are possible.

What I have learned through my trials is that every crisis forces us to redirect our lives. We are handed a cross, designed especially for us, and are asked to choose. We cannot choose whether we will take the cross. No. The cross is ours to bear no matter what. But we can freely choose how we respond to it.

Do we accept that cross and prayerfully carry it to its completion? Or do we try to cast it aside, cursing it when it does disappear, cursing it as it grows in weight? I have tried both responses to my crosses, and I can assure you that while cursing those things in our lives that cause us to suffer may feel like the more natural thing to do, embracing our suffering is by far the easier response to make, because it is the only response that coincides with God's will.

St. Alphonsus de Ligouri gifted the Church Militant with a short work entitled <u>Uniformity with God's Will</u>. In this document, he not only lays out the joys of surrendering one's will to Our Lord, but gives us five ways in which to practice this surrender. I have included these five basic steps below, but highly recommend you acquire a copy of the entire document, which is available in the public domain and can be readily found online.

> *1. In external matters. In times of great heat, cold or rain; in times of famine, epidemics, and similar occasions we should refrain from expressions like these: "What unbearable heat!" "What piercing cold!" "What a tragedy!" In these instances we should avoid expressions indicating opposition to God's will. We should want things to be just as they are, because it is God who thus disposes them. An incident in point would be this one: Late one night St. Francis Borgia arrived unexpectedly at a Jesuit house, in a snowstorm. He knocked and knocked on the door, but all to no purpose because the community being asleep, no one heard him. When morning came all were embarrassed for the discomfort he had experienced by having had to spend the night in the open. The saint, however, said he had enjoyed the greatest consolation during those*

long hours of the night by imagining that he saw our Lord up in the sky dropping the snowflakes down upon him.

2. In personal matters. In matters that affect us personally, let us acquiesce in God's will. For example, in hunger, thirst, poverty, desolation, loss of reputation, let us always say: "Do thou build up or tear down, O Lord, as seems good in thy sight. I am content. I wish only what thou dost wish." Thus too, says Rodriguez, should we act when the devil proposes certain hypothetical cases to us in order to wrest a sinful consent from us, or at least to cause us to be interiorly disturbed. For example: "What would you say or what would you do if some one were to say or do such and such a thing to you?" Let us dismiss the temptation by saying: "By God's grace, I would say or do what God would want me to say or do." Thus we shall free ourselves from imperfection and harassment.

3. Let us not lament if we suffer from some natural defect of body or mind; from poor memory, slowness of understanding, little ability, lameness or general bad health. What claim have we, or what obligation is God under, to give us a more brilliant mind or a more robust body? Who is ever offered a gift and then lays down the conditions upon which he will accept it? Let us thank God for what, in his pure goodness, he has given us and let us be content too with the manner in which he has given it to us.

Who knows? Perhaps if God had given us greater talent, better health, a more personable appearance, we might have lost our souls! Great talent and knowledge have caused many to be puffed up with the idea of their own importance and, in their pride, they have despised others. How easily those who have these gifts fall into grave danger to their salvation! How many on account of physical beauty or robust health have plunged headlong into a life of debauchery! How many, on the contrary, who, by reason of poverty, infirmity or physical deformity, have become saints and have saved their souls, who, given health, wealth or physical attractiveness had else lost their souls! Let us then be content with what God has given us. "But one thing is necessary," and it is not beauty, not health, not talent. It is the salvation of our immortal souls.

4. It is especially necessary that we be resigned in corporal infirmities. We should willingly embrace them in the manner and for the length of time that God wills. We ought to make use of the ordinary remedies in time of sickness—such is God's will; but if they are not effective, let us unite ourselves to God's will and this will be better for us than would be our restoration to health.

Let us say: "Lord, I wish neither to be well nor to remain sick; I want only what thou wilt." Certainly, it is more virtuous not to repine in times of painful illness; still and all, when our sufferings are excessive, it is not wrong to let our friends know what we are enduring, and also to ask God to free us from our sufferings. Let it be understood, however, that the sufferings here referred to are actually excessive. It often happens that some, on the occasion of a slight illness, or even a slight indisposition, want the whole world to stand still and sympathize with them in their illnesses.

But where it is a case of real suffering, we have the example of our Lord, who, at the approach of his bitter passion, made known his state of soul to his disciples, saying: "My soul is sorrowful even unto death" and besought his eternal Father to deliver him from it: "Father, if it be possible, let this chalice pass from me." But our Lord likewise taught us what we should do when we have made such a petition, when he added: "Nevertheless, not as I will, but as thou wilt."

I encourage you to practice these steps and instill them in the hearts of your family members, that no amount of future suffering may be wasted. Use these steps as points for frequent discussions. Analyze stories you hear on the news and discuss how things might be different if more souls embraced God's will. Challenge them to picture themselves in situations of great suffering and find what good God might want to come of it. Examine periods of suffering your family has endured in the past. What good came of it? What lessons were learned? What virtues were strengthened and why? Were any vices strengthened during this time? Could a stronger trust in God's love have prevented the additional suffering that came your way through these vices?

I also encourage you to discuss ways you can practice little mortifications throughout the day to further defeat your own will. Or at least be more mindful of the multitude of opportunities that present themselves at any moment. Ask yourself: As I dish out chicken breasts to my family members, do I keep the best one for myself? Or do I give it to the child I had just clashed with a few moments before? I have wandered into the pantry for the twelfth time this morning—do I really need to eat another handful or raisins or can I mortify my tendency to habitually snack for love of God? I have decided not to purchase a few items in my cart. I could leave them on a miscellaneous shelf in the store for someone else to put away. Or I can say, "For love of You, Lord," as I place each item back where it belongs.

There are so many ways in which we can mortify our wills. Every effort we make to do so builds the spiritual muscles we need to bear the crosses that come our way. We should strive to be so practiced in self mortification that we can joyfully say "Thy will be done" when faced with pain. Such acceptance pleases Our Lord immensely, for it is in those moments that we join our hearts with His as He suffered His Passion and proclaim to Him that our love for Him outweighs our love of self.

I pray that Fulton will one day find a way to use his story as a magnification of Almighty God and how He lovingly calls each of us to carry our cross with dignity befitting all who are called to reside in His Kingdom. My prayer for you is that you too will open your heart to your cross and allow it to bring you closer to God, to cherish it as a priceless gift that will perfect your soul. Just as Christ's Passion draws hearts to love Him more, may you draw others closer to Our Lord through your suffering. Praise His name through your pain, that God may be glorified through you! It is a difficult task, but one filled with joy and peace.

When I first read the book A Trustful Surrender to Divine Providence, it was for me the real beginning of my conversion. I was completely on fire with love for Our Lord and wanted to give Him the ultimate gift: my will, a complete abandonment of my own will that God's will be done. It was a tall order, for I am still very much in love with worldly ways in many areas of my life. Nevertheless, I was so inspired, I actually tried to give up my will completely for Lent. It lasted for about three hours, which made me realize how difficult yet powerful this sort of sacrifice could be. Accepting that I was not yet strong enough to give up my will completely, I decided to use this book as my daily meditation, working at chipping away at my will in smaller pieces.

I also turned to the works of the Saints. The Saints' writings revealed to me that vast chasm that separated me from Our Lord and showed me how to build a bridge of hope. I devoured these books, absorbing all I could, slowly filling those empty holes within my heart that still needed filling, teaching me more of what it means to be loved by God and how the best way to respond to that love was through the innumerable little moments God gives us throughout the day.

But just as we should strive for a mortified heart, know that failures will be frequent. Be gentle with yourself when you stumble. Embrace the humility that comes with such failings and offer up your pride to Our Lord. Know that in many ways, we learn more about ourselves through our failings than we do our successes.

One time, I was severely tempted to eat a Twinkie, of all things (yeah, I know. I am not even sure how it made its way into our house), and my usual "I offer up this temptation and refuse this Twinkie for love of You" was just not working. So, I pulled out all the stops. I thought of all the souls in Purgatory. I thought of all the mothers agonizing over their decision whether to have an abortion or not. I imagined souls in their last agony, requiring just one more sacrifice to move them towards perfect contrition. I placed that Twinkie on the altar in our prayer room, offering my sacrifice for whomever needed it most, closed the door, and returned to my housework.

Unfortunately, unlike most days when I was sorely tempted, I was unable to let this Twinkie go. For the next hour, all I could think about was that Twinkie. Golden, fluffy cake, creamy sweet filling. I caved. I flung open the door to the prayer room, grabbed the Twinkie and ate it in the bathroom, consuming my precious cake, letting every soul in the world fend for themselves.

Egads, I had a lot of work to do! But even in this embarrassing failure, I learned a few things. Sometimes prayer and a good intention is not enough. Most times I am weaker than I like to admit. And Twinkies are not nearly as good as I remembered them being as a child.

***

It is Your ardent desire that we arrive safely before You when our work here on Earth is through. Therefore, strengthen me in virtue however You see fit. We thank You, Lord, for the multitude of little ways You present to us throughout the day to practice surrendering our wills to You. Please be generous with Your challenges, but even more generous with Your forgiveness when we fall. Amen.

CHAPTER 24

"I am definitively loved and whatever happens to me—I am awaited by this Love. And so my life is good."
—*St. Josephine Bakhita*

Fulton had just returned from a trip to Galveston, where he had surgery on his mouth. Our son, post-surgery, is never a pretty sight, and so whenever he has surgery, the attention is increased. As we were walking into a restaurant, a woman came running to Fulton and collapsed at his feet in tears. "I am sorry to do this, but I saw you in the parking lot and I just had to tell you that God has big plans for you! He loves you so much! The Lord will do great things through you and you will change many hearts!"

Fulton was rather surprised by this woman's violent reaction to him, so I calmly stepped in. "Thank you so much. God does have special plans for my son." I handed her a card. "Would you please pray for him?"

The woman calmed down a bit, assured us of her prayers, and left. When we returned home, I asked Fulton, "Do you know what she meant when she said that God will do great things through you?"

"No," he answered.

"Well, sometimes God uses people to help Him teach others about Him. He wants everyone to know how much He loves them and chooses certain people to be His special messengers. Remember how Jesus died on the Cross? Why did He do that?"

"Because He loves us."

"That's right! But some people do not know the story of how much Jesus loves us, so He uses other people to teach them. When you do your Brave Breaths, or tell people that God is fixing you, or hand out burn cards, you are giving people hope, because if they see a little boy being so brave and so happy, they know that they can also be brave and happy through their suffering too, as long as they remember to love God and offer it up for His glory. The woman believes that you will be able to make many hearts love God because of the suffering you have gone through. Maybe she is right. When you get older, maybe you will be better able to understand why all this has happened to you and what God needs you to do for Him." On and on I droned about redemptive suffering, God's greater glory and other miscellaneous pieces of information I thought would help him understand. And just to make sure I was getting through to him, I asked, "Now do you understand?"

Fulton's eyes had glazed over minutes before. "Not really . . ."

So be it. He was not even in kindergarten, after all. But the question kept returning.

"Mama, why did I get burned?"

I knew what he was asking, but he was only four years old. I just didn't think he would be ready for the answer at such a young age.

As I sat by his bedside every day during those first few weeks, I had a lot of time to think about how we would handle the various difficult stages that lay ahead. Once I understood how the accident happened, I was presented with an additional quandary. Fulton needed his father to help him deal with his injuries as much as he needed me. And I knew that as he grew, he would need the influence of a masculine role to help him deal with the more difficult struggles that would come. To blame Jay for the accident would have set up a wall between them that could take years to tear back down. Truth was important, but the way it was told was crucial.

In the beginning, we skipped past the deeper meaning behind suffering and focused on, "It was a very sad accident." As he progressed, he wanted to know more details. "Daddy made a mistake and he is so very sorry. Our hearts cry about what happened to you all the time." This was always coupled with an explanation that Daddy saved him.

Fulton has always been fascinated with the fact that God has given him his very own Guardian Angel, so we used this to help him get a better understanding of what happened that day. "After the explosion," we explained, "your Guardian Angel told Daddy's Guardian Angel that you needed help. His angel told him you were in danger and Daddy ran to you . . ."

"And he went 'OOOF!'" Fulton always flails his arms around and expresses great joy in the thought of his father tackling him onto the ground to smother the flames. "Daddy saved me!" The story always ends there for him, and we move on to other little boy topics.

That approach was the simplest, but one that would not always be enough. I knew how much Fulton would need God to see him through as he grew. How does one explain the permissive will of God to a four-year-old without making God sound like a monster?

Fulton and I were holding on to each other, skating on thin ice, and I prayed He would guide me and keep us safe. "I accept this cross, Lord, but please give me the wisdom to help Fulton carry his."

One night, I was massaging his scars as he was lying in bed, and once again the question came up. "Mama, why was I burned?" I still hadn't gotten used to the question, and my heart ached for my son.

"Well, honey," I softly answered, "it was a terrible accident. But God is fixing you a little more every day, and we all love you so much. And that helps you get better, too."

"But why was I burned?" he asked again.

Knowing he was not going to stand for the typical 'accidents happen' talk yet again, I decided to dive in. "Well," I began slowly, "sometimes things happen to us that we do not understand very well in the beginning. We think that they are terrible things. And we are right. But sometimes there are also wonderful things that come with the bad stuff. And if the bad stuff never happened, then the good stuff never would have happened either."

"Like meeting Miss Heather?"

I smiled. "That's right! Maybe it was important to God that we met Miss Heather. And that you got to teach the doctors and nurses about Brave Breaths so they can teach the other children. And how you remind everyone that God is fixing you. Do you think those things make God happy?"

He nodded.

"Me too. God gives us everything we need to love Him and to teach others to love Him. He has taken very good care of us. So, to show Him we love Him and that we are thankful He takes such good care of us, maybe we can make some good happen from the bad stuff and make God happy."

It was not a perfect answer, but in my defense, I still do not truly know why he was burned, either. All I could do at that point was give it up to the Lord and trust that He knew what He was doing as I watched and hoped for signs that Fulton was on the right track.

Then about two years ago, I was reading one of the Treasure Box books, a beautiful series printed by TAN Books, to him. We have read these books several times, and Fulton's favorite part is the ongoing, very enjoyable Wupsy story. It is a story of a Guardian Angel named Wupsy and his little boy Sunny. Aside from the beautiful way Guardian Angels are portrayed in this series, Fulton likes how Wupsy's worship is described. Whenever Wupsy is thankful or has an urgent prayer, he bows his head and "loves God hard"—a concept Fulton grasped immediately and would always express with tightly closed eyes and hard-clasped hands.

On this particular day he wanted me to read one of the first books again. I had not read the beginning of these stories since before the accident, so I was startled when I read the following passage:

> *"One day Sunny was making mud pies, but after a while he got tired of that and looked around for something else to play with. Something bright and snapping and jumping caught his eye. A fire! His mother had just put the dinner on and had turned around for just one minute to swat at a beetle. In that one little minute, Sunny toddled over to the fire and reached out to catch the pretty flames.*
>
> *Now Wupsy was watching Sunny and he was just about to call him away from the fire with an angel song, when he heard God speak.*
>
> *God said, "Let Sunny go."*
>
> *Now Wupsy was an Angel, so he understood what God meant. He knew that God might let Sunny get hurt a little, but it would come out all right.*
>
> *Sunny leaned over, trying to catch the pretty flames, and what do you think happened? He fell right into the fire! He began to scream."*

Lots of things were going on in my head as I read these pages. *What a frightening thing to tell a child! How did this not bother me before the accident!* But then I continued on.

> *"Ya-WAH!!! YA! WA! YA-WA-WA-WA!"*
>
> *His mother, Ntaka-Ntaka, turned around and grabbed Sunny from the fire. She wrapped a big piece of cloth around him to put out the flames. Poor Sunny! He was terribly burned. It hurt awfully.*
>
> *Wupsy was still feeling very sorry for Sunny, but he knew God was going to do something nice so he stopped worrying.*
>
> *Ntaka-Ntaka got a wooden bowl full of oil and poured it over Sunny. That felt better. Sunny grew very quiet and seemed to be asleep.*
>
> *Suddenly Wupsy heard God whispering to him and he listened very carefully.*
>
> *Wupsy smiled a beautiful angel smile. He clapped his hands. He was so excited. He had known it all along! God was going to do something wonderful. He bowed down his wings and loved God hard for a few seconds, then jumped up and flew off."*

Wupsy was obviously concerned for Sunny's safety, but God had a bigger plan. Would Fulton somehow identify with this higher plan? Could a mere child grasp its significance?

Somehow, even on the day of the accident, I grasped the fact that as long as we remained firm in our faith, whatever God had planned, it would be for the betterment of Fulton's soul and perhaps the souls of others. So I trusted. But how do you explain the mysteries of God to a child? All you can do is pray that someday this message sinks in and transforms a heart from pain to glory.

So, as I read the words of his bedtime story aloud I thought, "Should I go on? What is he thinking about this scene? Will he build a barrier between himself and God because of this or will he one day learn to accept God's permissive will?"

My question was immediately answered. For as these very thoughts were going through my head, and as I was reading the above page out loud, Fulton sat up and said excitedly, "Oh! Now I understand!"

"You understand what, Honey?"

"Why I got burned."

Ah-ha! "And why do you think you got burned?"

He paused a moment, as if considering what was just revealed to him. Then he sighed and said, "You don't understand." He nestled back under my arm and pointed to the book—his signal to continue on with the story.

And so it goes. We as a family continue on with this story, each taking it in with our own perspectives, gleaning from it all we can. We do not have a perfect understanding of what has happened in our lives—that is for God alone to know. My very own St. Theresa of Avila once said, "If you seek to carry no other crosses but those whose reason you understand, perfection is not for you." I am at peace with this fact. While complete understanding may never be ours to possess, what He does want us to understand is this: He loves with a love so powerful, He chose ultimate suffering for our sakes. And He will always give to us only that which will ultimately bring us to Eternal Joy.

This alone is enough to make me "bow down and love God hard" in gratitude that our Father forever does all that He can to save us. Thy will be done, Lord. Thy will be done.

***

An Act of Abandonment
Thanks be to thee, my Lord Jesus Christ, for all the benefits thou hast given
me, for all the pains and insults thou hast borne for me. O most merciful
redeemer, friend and brother, may I know thee more clearly, love thee more
dearly, and follow thee more nearly, day by day. Amen.
—Prayer of Saint Richard of Chichester

Epilogue

"Be merry, really merry. The life of a true Christian should be a perpetual jubilee, a prelude to the festivals of eternity."
—*St. Theophane Venard*

I saw an ad for the Wounded Warrior Project the other day. As the ad played, they showed soldiers with various injuries dealing with 'real life' after their life changing event. One soldier, in particular, caught my eye. He was getting dressed for the day, but because of his severe burn injuries, one of the things he had to 'put on' was his ears.

Fulton's ears (or lack thereof) is kind of a topic we haven't hit head on yet with him. He knows his hearing is not very good, and that his ears are 'very small'. Cleaning them is vastly different from the way it used to be, since his scars have created a few deep pockets in the ear area that require regular attention in addition to his regular ear canals. He has taken this all in stride, and honestly, unless we are washing his hair, we are pretty much at the point where we do not notice that his head is missing a few accessories. Which was why this commercial caught my attention.

The physical therapists at Shriners had mentioned that as he grows he will be getting some ears. And sometimes when we are getting him scanned for his face masks, I will see various prosthetic body parts on the counter, awaiting their final fittings.

And I wonder—how will Fulton feel about having fake ears? Will years of not having them and dealing with the stares break his confidence down? Should we get them sooner, if possible? And how on earth do those things stay in place, anyway?

Later that day, I mentioned to Fulton that I saw a soldier on TV who was burned like he was. "And you will never guess what he had to put on as he was getting dressed for the day!"

"What?" he asked, only half interested.

"He put on," *what was I doing bringing this up right now?* "a pair," *are you kidding me, Cassandra? Why are you telling him this?* "of EARS!"

Would we have a detailed conversation about why someone would want prosthetic ears? Would he suddenly become self conscious about his own ears? Would he start asking questions to which I did yet know the answers? As I finished the sentence, panic hit me, and I wondered why I even brought it up in the first place. I awaited his response . . .

"BWA-HAHAHAHAHAHA!"

His entire face contorted as only his face can, laughing. Laughing so much, in fact, his eyes started to tear up. And off he ran. "Hey Shannon!" he called. "Guess what! There was a soldier who was burned and he had to put on his ears! HAHAHAHAHAHA! Someday I'm gonna get ears, too, and you can watch me put them on! HAHAHAHAHA!" This, of course, was followed by various demonstrations of how the ears probably are attached, and each sibling joined in the creativity of the moment.

Good grief—this child is laughing at himself!

And then I smiled. Could it be, this is the way Our Lord wants us to look at our ourselves and the trials we face? To not get bogged down with the downside of it all to the point where it paralyzes and prevents God's glory to shine through, but instead focus on what joy can come of it?

To be humble enough to laugh at oneself takes courage. It leaves you exposed. Vulnerable. But when, out of a deep love of God, you embrace the cross with which you have been blessed, a transformation takes place within your heart that allows you to not only accept your flaws and your burdens, but take joy in them and spread that joy to others. Your struggles are transformed into a source of sanctification and become the vehicle by which you ultimately give God glory in Heaven.

Fulton's journey has only just begun. I have been warned that at any time, the effects of his injuries and appearance can suddenly take a turn for him emotionally and darker days may be ahead. But for now, we are building on the joys at hand. He has accepted what has happened to him as part of God's bigger plan for his life. He brings joy to others through his cross. He embraces his role as one who serves as a warning to others to be careful around fire. He inspires. He renews people's faith. And he laughs. A lot. Which immediately puts others at ease and helps others laugh, too.

As I pondered this, I noticed the children had redirected the conversation from how to get the ears on to the multitude of ways the ears might come off. "And maybe," Fulton was giggling, "I can be on a roller coaster and they will fly off my head because I am riding so fast!"

At this point, all of us were laughing so hard, tears were streaming down our faces. Dear Lord, this child brings us so much joy!

***

Thank you, Lord, for showing me how to find the joy mingled within our sorrows. Help me to embrace each and every challenge You permit me to face. Remind me of the joy found in them. And give me humility to perhaps even laugh as I struggle to overcome the things You have given me for the betterment of my soul. Amen.

ABOUT THE AUTHOR

Cassandra Poppe has written for several online Catholic websites; most notably CatholicMom.com. She is a member of the Catholic Writers Guild, author of The Rosary Quilt religious program, contributor to The Catholic Mom's Prayer Companion, and occasionally dabbles in blogging as time permits.

She is a converted, Traditional Catholic wife and mother of 7 who delves deeply into the mysteries of God's great mercy through her writing. She works out her salvation with fear and trembling among the liturgy, laundry, love and laughter as it all unfolds within the humble walls of her domestic church, and enjoys sharing her experiences through her writing and as a public speaker.

Made in the USA
Middletown, DE
28 January 2017